AQA English an English Language

Foundation Tier

Teacher's Book

GCSE

Jo Mulliner
Malcolm Seccombe
Marian Slee
Julia Waines
Malcolm J. White

Series Editor

Imelda Pilgrim

Nelson Thornes

Published in 2010 by:
Nelson Thornes Ltd
Delta Place
27 Bath Road
CHELTENHAM
GL53 7TH
United Kingdom

10 11 12 13 14 / 10 9 8 7 6 5 4 3 2

A catalogue record for this book is available from the British Library

ISBN 978 1 4085 0601 1

Cover photograph: Heather Gunn Photography

Page make-up by OKS Prepress Services Pvt Ltd

Printed and bound in Croatia by Zrinski

Contents

Introducing the new specs

Introduction

The introduction of a new specification is a worrying time for any teacher and subject department. Initially, everything seems different and it takes time to familiarise yourself with what you need to do in order to ensure your teaching meets the requirements of the specification and your students fulfil their potential. This section of the Teacher's Book is designed to help you understand the demands of the new specifications, and the chapters that follow, when used in conjunction with the relevant Student Book, are intended to help you to teach the specifications effectively.

The choices

The first step is to decide which specification your students will study. There are two options:

GCSE English

Unit 1: Understanding and producing non-fiction texts

External exam (80 marks, 40 per cent in total):

- Section A – Reading (1 hour, 40 marks)
- Section B – Writing (1 hour, 40 marks)

Unit 2: Speaking and listening

Controlled assessment (45 marks, 20 per cent in total):

- Presenting (15 marks)
- Discussing and listening (15 marks)
- Roleplaying (15 marks)

Unit 3: Understanding and producing creative texts

Controlled assessment (90 marks, 40 per cent in total):

- Part A – Understanding creative texts: literary reading (up to 4 hours, 45 marks)
- Part B – Producing creative texts: creative writing (up to 4 hours, 45 marks)

GCSE English Language

Unit 1: Understanding and producing non-fiction texts

External exam (80 marks, 40 per cent in total):

- Section A – Reading (1 hour, 40 marks)
- Section B – Writing (1 hour, 40 marks)

Unit 2: Speaking and listening

Controlled assessment (45 marks, 20 per cent in total):

- Presenting (15 marks)
- Discussing and listening (15 marks)
- Role-playing (15 marks)

Unit 3: Understanding spoken and written texts and writing creatively

Controlled assessment (80 marks, 40 per cent in total):

- Part A – Extended reading (up to 4 hours, 30 marks)
- Part B – Creative writing (up to 4 hours, 30 marks)
- Part C – Spoken language study (up to 3 hours, 20 marks)

As you can see, both specifications are exactly the same with regard to Units 1 and 2. However, they differ considerably in Unit 3:

- GCSE English covers the requirements for reading in the National Curriculum. GCSE English Language does not. Students taking GCSE English Language must also study, and take an exam in, GCSE English Literature.
- GCSE English Language offers the opportunity to study spoken English. This is not a requirement of GCSE English.

How to make a choice

Many centres currently enter all students for both English and English Literature and will wish to continue this practice. In such cases, GCSE English Language is the obvious option. Others may decide that one GCSE qualification is appropriate and choose GCSE English. A third option is to choose GCSE English Language for some students and GCSE English for others. Fundamentally, the choices departments make will very much depend on the students they teach, their needs and the needs of the centre.

Assessment Objectives

The first place to start with any specification is the Assessment Objectives. These underpin the areas for study and provide the focus for the testing and assessment of these areas. There is considerable overlap between the Assessment Objectives for GCSE English and those for GCSE English Language and some significant differences. The numbering and the naming of the different areas is initially confusing when looking at the specifications together. The details below are intended to clarify this.

GCSE English: AO1 Speaking and listening

GCSE English Language: AO1 Speaking and listening

- Speak to communicate clearly and purposefully; structure and sustain talk, adapting it to different situations and audiences; use standard English and a variety of techniques as appropriate.
- Listen and respond to speakers' ideas and perspectives, and how they construct and express meanings.
- Interact with others, shaping meanings through suggestions, comments and questions and drawing ideas together.
- Create and sustain different roles.

GCSE English Language: AO2 Study of spoken language

- Understand variations in spoken language, explaining why language changes in relation to contexts.
- Evaluate the impact of spoken language choices in their own and others' use.

GCSE English: AO2 Reading

GCSE English Language: AO3 Studying written language

- Read and understand texts, selecting material appropriate to purpose, collating from different sources and making comparisons and cross-references as appropriate.
- Develop and sustain interpretations of writers' ideas and perspectives.
- Explain and evaluate how writers use linguistic, grammatical, structural and presentational features to achieve effects and engage and influence the reader.
- Understand texts in their social, cultural and historical contexts. **[GCSE English only]**

GCSE English: AO3 Writing

GCSE English Language: AO4 Writing

- Write [to communicate] clearly, effectively and imaginatively, using and adapting forms and selecting vocabulary appropriate to task and purpose in ways that engage the reader.
- Organise information and ideas into structured and sequenced sentences, paragraphs and whole texts, using a variety of linguistic and structural features to support cohesion and overall coherence.
- Use a range of sentence structures for clarity, purpose and effect, with accurate punctuation and spelling.

The Assessment Objectives are intended for teachers. They define the skills that students need to develop and will be required to demonstrate. Clearly students need to know what these skills are. Most students are, however, unable to readily access the specialist language of the Assessment Objectives, a term such as 'to support cohesion and overall coherence' having little real meaning for them. The Student Book uses more accessible language to explain the requisite skills to students and, at various stages, 'unpick' the Assessment Objectives in detail (see pages 83–4).

Areas of overlap between Language and Literature

A quick look at the AOs for GCSE English Literature reveals the extent to which they overlap with those for its partner subject, GCSE English Language. The areas of overlap are highlighted below:

- **AO1:** Respond to texts critically and imaginatively; select and evaluate relevant textual detail to illustrate and support interpretations.

- **AO2:** Explain how language, structure and form contribute to writers' presentation of ideas, themes and settings.

- **AO3:** Make comparisons and explain links between texts, evaluating writers' different ways of expressing meaning and achieving effects.

- **AO4:** Relate texts to their social, cultural and historical contexts; explain how texts have been influential and significant to self and other readers in different contexts and at different times.

Quality of Written Communication (QWC). Candidates must:

- Ensure that text is legible and that spelling, punctuation and grammar are accurate so that the meaning is clear.

- Select and use a form and style of writing appropriate to purpose and to complex subject matter.

- Organise information clearly and coherently, using specialist vocabulary when relevant.

This demonstrates the extent to which the skills you are developing in your students for GCSE English Language are directly transferrable to GCSE English Literature.

Introducing and using the Nelson Thornes resources

Nelson Thornes and AQA

Nelson Thornes has worked in partnership with AQA to ensure that the Student Book, the Teacher's Book and the accompanying online resources offer you the best support possible for your teaching of the GCSE course. The print and online resources together **unlock blended learning**; this means that the links between the activities in the book and the activities online blend together to maximise students' understanding of a topic and help them to achieve their potential.

All AQA-endorsed resources undergo a thorough quality assurance process to ensure that their contents closely match the AQA specification. You can be confident that the content of materials branded with AQA's 'Exclusively Endorsed' logo have been written, checked and approved by AQA senior examiners, in order to achieve AQA's exclusive endorsement.

Student Book

Reading, writing, and speaking and listening – as all teachers of English know – are not distinct and separate entities: reading enhances writing; speaking and listening enable a better understanding of reading, and so on.

The Student Book has been divided into four sections, with a predominant focus on a given area to demonstrate clear coverage of the Assessment Objectives and for clarity of organisation:

- Reading
- Writing
- Speaking and listening
- Spoken language.

However, all sections contain elements of the other areas: for example, reading chapters are interspersed with writing and speaking and listening activities, developing students' skills not only in understanding texts but in articulating that understanding. This is essential if students are to effectively express their response to reading in an exam or controlled assessment situation.

Each section of the Student Book concludes with exam and/or controlled assessment chapters. These chapters draw together the skills developed throughout the section and show students how to apply them in their assessments.

All Student Book chapters include:

A list of student-friendly learning objectives at the start of the chapter that contain targets linked to the requirements of the specification.

Activities to develop and reinforce the skills focus for the lesson.

A list of points at the end of the chapter that summarise what students have covered.

Some (but not all) chapters feature:

Biographies and backgrounds provide students with additional information about a writer or a text.

Terms students will find it useful to be able to define and understand. The definitions also appear in the glossary at the end of the Student Book.

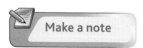

Useful points for students to keep a note of, for example, planning or revision hints.

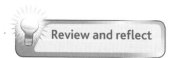

Opportunities for peer and/or self-assessment.

Specific activities testing speaking and listening skills.

Stretch yourself

Extension activities to take the work in a chapter further.

Top tip

Guidance from the examiners or moderators on how to avoid common pitfalls and mistakes, and how to achieve the best marks in the exam or controlled assessment.

The texts and activities in the Student Book have been chosen by the writers to appeal to students, but no single textbook or set of teacher notes can account for the wide range of young people encountered in the classroom. It is the combination of a good teacher and a good textbook that makes the latter most effective. You know your students best. Be prepared to use the materials in the Student Book selectively, to introduce your own texts and activities and to add explanation or differentiated criteria. In this way you will best suit the needs of the students who sit in front of you, and maximise the potential of the Student Book.

Teacher's Book

The Student Book provides a structured route for the development of the skills denoted by the Assessment Objectives. The Teacher's Book acts as a guide to the Student Book, drawing your attention to specific points of focus, providing answers to and guidance on the activities, and suggesting alternative approaches and possible extension work. It is not intended to be in any way prescriptive.

Each section of the Teacher's Book follows the order of the Student Book and includes chapter-by-chapter guidance on using the Student Book resources. It is not, however, essential that you follow the order of the chapters, and it is anticipated that teachers will create their own order from which to work through the chapters, moving between the sections to ensure variation in the primary focus on reading, writing, speaking and listening, and spoken language study.

In addition to the chapter-by-chapter coverage, each section also contains at the start:

- an overview of the section and the AOs
- a resources overview listing all the activities in the Student Book, along with the worksheets and interactive resources available online in *kerboodle!*
- a student checklist, which can be used to assess knowledge and understand before, during or after working through a section; it also indicates which chapters of the Student Book might be useful for consolidation of that particular skill
- a range of activities from the Student Book that can be used to assess student progress through the section
- a list of general resources that could be used to develop the teaching and learning from that section.

To enable you to track your coverage of the specifications, and to build in links with the AQA GCSE English Literature specification and Functional English standards, the grids on pages xiv–xvi provide full coverage of where the units of the specification are taught. In addition, some possible routes through the materials are suggested on pages x–xii.

Online resources

The online resources are available on *kerboodle!*, which can be accessed via the internet at www.kerboodle.com live, anytime, anywhere. If your school or college subscribes to *kerboodle!* you will be provided with your own personal log-in details. Once logged in, you can access your course and locate the required activity.

Throughout the Student Book and Teacher's Book, you will see a *k!* icon whenever there is a relevant interactive activity available in *kerboodle!*. Also within *kerboodle!* you will find chapter-by-chapter guidance on how to use each interactive activity, along with additional worksheets to enhance the material from the Student Book.

Please visit http://kerboodle.helpserve.com if you would like more information and help on how to use *kerboodle!*.

Finding a route through the materials

The chapters in this book can be used flexibly with students. However, you might find the following notes useful, in conjunction with the matching grids on pages xiii–xvi, to help you decide which units will meet particular teaching and learning targets and which will most appeal to your students.

Section A: Reading

The order of the chapters in the Reading section has been carefully planned so that students can follow a route of clear progression through the Assessment Objectives. However, the chapters can be grouped to reinforce particular skills as and when required. Some suggested groupings are given below:

Suggested grouping	Skills reinforced
Chapter 2: Making an impact Chapter 3: Engaging stories Chapter 4: Evaluating texts	These chapters all focus on analysis and evaluation of linguistic, grammatical, structural and presentation features, and how writers use these to engage and influence their readers.
Chapter 5: The time and the place	This chapter develops the Unit 3 requirement to 'understand texts in their social, cultural and historical context' and focuses particularly on literary texts.
Chapter 6: Creating a story	This chapter can be used to develop student's abilities to develop and sustain detailed comments on texts. They also focus on analysis and evaluation of linguistic, grammatical and structural features, and how writers use these to engage and influence their readers.
Chapter 7: Understanding arguments Chapter 8: Responding to texts Chapter 9: Exploring the writer's viewpoint	These chapters can be used to develop students' abilities to develop and sustain detailed comments. They also reinforce the importance of interpreting the texts and using evidence to support these interpretations.
Chapter 10: Comparing texts	This chapter looks in particular at the skill of comparing texts.

Section B: Writing

As with Reading, the order of chapters in Writing has been carefully thought through to ensure that students have a clear route through the skills and opportunities for progress checking.

Suggested grouping	Skills reinforced
Chapter 13: Communicate clearly Chapter 15: Building paragraphs Chapter 17: Different sentences	These chapters provide opportunities for students to practise writing in a range of sentence structures; to punctuate their sentences correctly; and to select sentences appropriate to their form, purpose and audience.
Chapter 14: Say what you mean Chapter 16: Word play Chapter 20: Adapting forms	These chapters all focus on adapting forms, vocabulary and linguistic features to suit audience and purpose.
Chapter 18: Writing non-fiction Chapter 19: Writing fiction	These chapters could be used as summative chapters in which students draw on their prior learning and skills to organise their ideas and information to write whole texts.

Section C: Speaking and listening

Specific guidance on speaking and listening skills is given in Section C, along with guidance on how this will be assessed. However, there are opportunities throughout the rest of the chapters to give students practice in speaking and listening. For example:

Links to other sections	Speaking and listening practice opportunities
Section A: Reading Chapter 10: Comparing texts	• Paired discussion on similarities and differences between two poems
Section B: Writing Chapter 15: Building paragraphs Chapter 21: Genres	• Paired discussion on the different ways to plan a piece of writing • Paired or group discussion to introduce the concept of genre
Section D: Spoken language Chapter 29: Understanding the influences Chapter 30: Multi-modal talk	• Group discussion on accents • Group discussion to establish the conventions of texting

In addition:

- many of the activities can be undertaken as paired work
- the Review and reflect activities can be done in pairs with students reviewing and assessing each other's work.

Section D: Spoken language

This section of the Student Book provides guidance on Unit 3, Part C of the English Language specification – the Spoken language study. Chapter 29 provides an introduction to thinking about the contexts of and influences on spoken language, whereas Chapter 30 focuses on the impact of new technologies on spoken language.

These chapters can be used as the basis for a discrete unit of work or can be linked to the other chapters, for example:

Chapters in other sections	Spoken language links
Section B: Writing Chapter 14: Say what you mean	• The analysis of the language used in text messages could be linked with multi-modal forms.
Section C: Speaking and listening Chapter 25: Presentation	• The segments on Standard English could be linked with considering how context, purpose and audience can affect spoken language.

Links to the AQA scheme of work

The following chapters can be used as starting points to support the scheme of work for Unit 1 published on the AQA website: http://web.aqa.org.uk/aqa-english-resource-zone

Topic outline	Relevant resources from the Student Book and *kerboodle!*
Approaching non-fiction texts	**Chapter 1: Finding information** Students identify key information and details in texts; select appropriate material to answer questions; explain how writers use words to affect their readers. **Chapter 15: Building paragraphs** Students think about how texts are organised and structured and how ideas and information are organised into sentences and paragraphs.
Features of non-fiction texts	**Chapter 2: Making an impact** Students investigate how texts are organised and think about the ways that presentational features are used for effect. **Chapter 14: Say what you mean** Students explore how language and form can be adapted to suit purpose and audience, including using emails and letters.

Topic outline	Relevant resources from the Student Book and kerboodle!
Close reading skills	**Chapter 3: Engaging stories** Students explore the language techniques used by writers and the effect these have on the reader. **Chapter 7: Understanding arguments** Students understand and explain the ideas expressed by writers; they examine how writers use language to influence their readers. **Chapter 16: Word play** Students use a range of vocabulary and think about how they will engage their audience through language choices. **Chapter 17: Different sentences** Students think about how they can match their sentence structures to their audience and purpose; and how they can use sentences to express their ideas, emphasise meaning and create effects.
Comparing texts	**Chapter 10: Comparing texts** Students study two texts, thinking about audience and purpose; use of presentation features; and use of language. They study the features of a written comparison and write their own comparison. **Chapter 18: Writing non-fiction** Students explore ways of planning, organising and structuring their non-fiction writing. **Chapter 21: Genres** Students practise writing in a range of genres.
Preparing for the examination	**Chapter 11: Making your reading skills count in the exam** Students learn how reading skills are tested in the exam, study texts and questions in a sample paper and consider how to improve their marks. **Chapter 22: Making your writing skills count in the exam** Students learn how their writing skills are tested in the exam, study questions in a sample paper, plan write and assess and answer; and review examiner's comments to find out how to achieve the best marks.

Links to the *AQA Anthology*

The skills required for English Literature Units 1A (Modern Texts), 2A (*Anthology*) and 5 (Exploring poetry) are built into and developed throughout the chapters of the *GCSE English and English Language Foundation Tier* Student Book. These are indicated in the matching grids on pages xiii–xvi.

However, the following chapters provide specific coverage of the texts from the *AQA Anthology*.

Poetry	**Chapter 5: The time and the place** This chapter provides analysis of 'Futility' both with and without contextual information. It also provides reflection on what impact understanding the context has. **Chapter 12: Making your reading skills count in the controlled assessment** Two poems from the Place cluster are used as the basis of the example question and answer: 'Below the Green Corrie' by Norman MacCaig and 'Storm in the Black Forest' by D.H. Lawrence. **Chapter 19: Writing fiction** Students analyse techniques used in *Brendon Gallacher* to create character.
Short stories	**Chapter 19: Writing fiction** Students explore techniques used in 'When the Wasps Drowned' to create character and to build tension.

Links to the set texts

As for the *AQA Anthology* texts, the skills required for the following GCSE English Literature units are built into and developed throughout the chapters of the *GCSE English and English Language Foundation Tier* Student Book:

- **Unit 1:** Exploring modern texts
- **Unit 3:** The significance of Shakespeare and the English Literary Heritage
- **Unit 4:** Approaching Shakespeare and the English Literary Heritage.

These are indicated in the matching grids on pages xiii–xvi.

Matching grids

The tables below outline how the resources link to the units of each of the specifications (English, English Language and English Literature), and the Functional English standards, and can be used when planning a scheme of work. In addition, they also indicate the texts types used and written; speaking and listening focus; spoken language focus. This information can be used to plan lessons and target particular student needs.

Section A: Reading

GCSE English: AO2 Reading GCSE English Language: AO3 Studying written language				
Chapter and AO focus	**English and English Language Units**	**Literature Units**	**Functional English standards**	**Text types used**
Chapter 1: Finding information • Read and understand texts, select material appropriate to purpose.	1A 3A	1 2 and 3/4 and 5	R1.1, 1.2, 1.3 R2.1, 2.2, 2.3	• Information texts • Marketing/information leaflets
Chapter 2: Making an impact • Explain how writers use structure and presentational features to achieve effects and to engage and influence the reader.	1A 3A	1 2 and 3/4 and 5	R1.1, 1.3 R2.3, 2.5	• Marketing/information leaflets
Chapter 3: Engaging stories • Explain how writers use linguistic, structural and presentational features to achieve effects and to engage and influence the reader.	1A 3A	1 2 and 3/4 and 5	R1.2, 1.3 R2.3, 2.5	• Novel • Play • Poetry • Advertisement
Chapter 4: Evaluating texts • Evaluate how writers use linguistic and presentational features to achieve effects and to engage and influence the reader.	1A 3A	1 2 and 3/4 and 5	R1.3 R2.3, 2.5	• Advertisement • Poster • Letter
Chapter 5: The time and the place • Understand texts in their social, cultural and historical context.	3A	1 3/4		• Advertisement • Poetry

Chapter and AO focus	English and English Language Units	Literature Units	Functional English standards	Text types used
Chapter 6: Creating a story • Explain and evaluate how writers use linguistic, grammatical and structural features to achieve effects and to engage and influence the reader. • Develop and sustain interpretations of writers' ideas and perspectives.	1A 3A		R2.5	• Student's short story
Chapter 7: Understanding arguments • Develop and sustain interpretations of writers' ideas and perspectives. • Explain and evaluate how writers use linguistic, grammatical, structural and presentational features to achieve effects and engage and influence the reader.	1A 3A		R2.4	• Newspaper articles
Chapter 8: Responding to texts • Develop interpretation of writers' ideas and perspectives.	1A 3A	1 2/4 and 5	R2.3, 2.4	• Travel guide • Film review • Magazine article
Chapter 9: Exploring the writer's viewpoint • Develop and sustain interpretation of writers' ideas and perspectives.	1A 3A	1 2/4 and 5	R2.3, 2.4	• Fiction • Biographical account • Poetry • Travel guide
Chapter 10: Comparing texts • Collate and make comparisons and cross reference as appropriate.	1A 3A	2 and 3/5	R2.5	• Advertisements • Marketing • Poetry

Section B: Writing

GCSE English: AO3 Writing
GCSE English Language: AO3 Studying written language

Chapter and AO focus	English and English Language units	Functional English standards	Text types written
Chapter 13: Communicate clearly • Write [to communicate] clearly and effectively in ways that engage the reader.	1B, 3B	W1.1, 1.4, 1.5 W2.1, 2.5, 2.6	• Sentences and paragraphs • Review
Chapter 14: Say what you mean • Use and adapt forms appropriate to task and purpose (focus on non-fiction forms).	1B, 3B	W1.3 W2.3	Persuasive text: • Magazine advertisement Informative text: • Postcard and instructions • Formal email • Letter of complaint
Chapter 15: Building paragraphs • Organise information and ideas into structured and sequenced sentences and paragraphs.	1B, 3B	W1.2 W2.2	• Essay plan • Instructional and informative text
Chapter 16: Word play • Select vocabulary appropriate to task and purpose.	1B, 3B	W1.3 W2.3	• Descriptive writing • Informative writing
Chapter 17: Different sentences • Use a range of sentence structures for clarity, purpose and effect.	1B, 3B	W1.2, 1.4, 1.5 W2.2, 2.4, 2.5, 2.6	• Simple and compound sentences • Dialogue • Biographical/diary entry
Chapter 18: Writing non-fiction • Organise information and ideas into whole texts, using a variety of linguistic features to support cohesion and overall coherence (non-fiction).	1B, 3B	W1.2 W2.2, 2.4	• Newspaper article • Editorial
Chapter 19: Writing fiction • Organise information and ideas into whole texts, using a variety of linguistic features to support cohesion and overall coherence (fiction).	3B		• Drama/play • Script/dialogue • Prose • Poetry
Chapter 20: Adapting forms • Use and adapt forms appropriate to task and purpose.	1B, 3B	W1.3 W2.3	• Review/descriptive text • Information text
Chapter 21: Genres • Use and adapt forms and select vocabulary appropriate to task and purpose.	1B, 3B	W1.3 W2.3	• Writing for openings for different genres

Section C: Speaking and listening

GCSE English: AO1 Speaking and listening
GCSE English Language: AO1 Speaking and listening

Chapter and AO focus	English and English Language units	Functional English standards	Speaking and listening focus
Chapter 24: Your speaking and listening skills • Speak to communicate clearly and purposefully; structure and sustain talk; use standard English and a variety of techniques as appropriate.	2	SL1.1, SL1.2, SL1.3, SL1.4 SL2.1, SL2.2, SL2.3, SL2.4	• Identifying features of good speakers and listeners • Using body language • Improving speaking and listening skills and setting targets
Chapter 25: Presentation • Speak to communicate clearly and purposefully; use Standard English and a variety of techniques as appropriate.	2	SL1.2, SL1.4 SL2.2, SL2.4	• Identifying features of good presentations and how to achieve them • Planning and rehearsing
Chapter 26: Discussing and listening • Interact with others, shaping meanings through suggestions, comments and questions and drawing ideas together.	2	SL1.1, SL1.2, SL1.3 SL2.1, SL2.3, SL2.4	• Working successfully in a group • Asking questions
Chapter 27: Role play • Create and sustain different roles.	2		• Using a character plan • Practising and performing • Giving feedback on role plays

Section D: Spoken language

GCSE English Language: AO2 Study of spoken language

Chapter and AO focus	English Language unit	Spoken language focus
Chapter 29 Understanding the influences • Understand variations in spoken language, explaining why language changes in relation to contexts. • Evaluate the impact of spoken language choices in their own and others' use.	3C	• Using language in different contexts • Accents, dialect and idiolect, influences of social groups on spoken language • Recording spoken language, preparing transcripts
Chapter 30 Multi-modal talk • Understand variations in spoken language, explaining why language changes in relation to contexts. • Evaluate the impact of spoken language choices in their own and others' uses.	3C	• Impact of technology on language • Language of text messages • Telephone conversations • Online communication

Section A: Reading

Overview

Section A of the Student Book is designed to develop students' skills in reading as defined by the Assessment Objectives for GCSE English (AO2 Reading) and GCSE English Language (AO3 Studying written language) and tested in the exam and the controlled assessments.

GCSE English: AO2 Writing

GCSE English Language: AO3 Studying written language

- Read and understand texts, selecting material appropriate to purpose, collating from different sources and making comparisons and cross-references as appropriate.

- Develop and sustain interpretations of writers' ideas and perspectives.

- Explain and evaluate how writers use linguistic, grammatical, structural and presentational features to achieve effects and engage and influence the reader.

- Understand texts in their social, cultural and historical contexts. [GCSE English only]

The chapters provide opportunities for students to draw on and revise the skills they have already acquired in reading, and to develop these further. The learning objectives, founded in the Assessment Objectives but in 'student-friendly' language, are given at the start of each chapter. Throughout each chapter the learning points are clarified and modelled, and followed by activities that are designed to reinforce and extend students' learning.

Students are encouraged to work independently or in pairs or small groups, as appropriate, and are given regular opportunities to assess their personal progress and that of other students, often against fixed criteria. The learning within the chapters is cumulative, building on what has come before, and at the end of several chapters there is a summative activity which challenges students to demonstrate their learning across the whole section.

Each chapter can be used as a discrete stand-alone topic with activities and tasks specific to the named objectives. They do not have to be done in the order in which they appear in the Student Book, though it is worth noting that this order was arrived at after careful consideration of how best to build students' skills in reading.

Assessment

GCSE English

External exam: Reading non-fiction texts (1 hour)

Controlled assessment: Understanding creative texts (up to 4 hours)

GCSE English Language

External exam: Reading non-fiction texts (1 hour)

Controlled assessment: Extended reading (up to 4 hours)

Nelson Thornes resources

Chapter	Student Book activities	kerboodle! resources
1: Finding information	1: Text marking to locate information in a text 2: Skimming a text to find answers to questions 3: Scanning a text to find answers to questions 4: Using organisational features to locate information in a text Check your learning: Recapping methods used to signpost information in a text	• Worksheet 1a: Car design • Worksheet 1b: Focus on the positives • Worksheet 1c: Smoke alarms • Learning activity: Skimming and scanning a website • Learning activity: Identifying text types • Webquest activity: Researching obesity
2: Making an impact	1: Matching information in a leaflet to its purpose 2: Using design clues to decide who the audience might be 3: Identifying how colours and pictures have been used in a leaflet 4: Identifying how words and text styles have been used in a leaflet 5: Analysing a sample student answer explaining how pictures have been used in the leaflet 6: Complete the student answer by adding a paragraph explaining how words and text have been used Check your learning: Examining presentational and structural features in a different leaflet	• Worksheet 2a: Purpose and audiences of the front cover • Worksheet 2b: Use of pictures and colour • Worksheet 2c: Use of words and fonts • Worksheet 2d: Writing about features 1 • Worksheet 2e: Writing about features 2 • Connecting comments activity: Analysing a web page • Learning activity: Analysing a website • Planning activity: Analysing an electronic text
3: Engaging stories	1: Selecting details from a prose text to find out more about a character 2–3: Using dialogue to find out more about a character; writing a paragraph to summarise learning, using details from the text 4: Selecting details from a prose text to find out more about setting 5: Working with a partner to select details about setting from a text; writing a paragraph to explain how the writer uses words to describe the setting 6: Suggesting reasons for a writer's choice of words to create mood; choosing different words that would alter the mood 7: Examining how a writer uses words to create tone	• Worksheet 3a: Characters 1 • Worksheet 3b: Characters 2 • Worksheet 3c: *Oliver Twist* • Worksheet 3d: Response to the short story opening • Worksheet 3e: 'The Park Hotel' • Planning activity: Creating characters • Viewpoints activity: *On My Own Two Feet* • Analysis activity: Setting the scene
4: Evaluating texts	1: Matching the purpose and audience to a text 2: Matching presentational and linguistic features to a text 3: Paired discussion of how the features of a text match the purpose and audience 4: Examining an image to look at the main presentational features and their effects and their impact they on the intended purpose and audience 5: Analysing a sample student answer on evaluating presentational features 6: Evaluating the effects of language used in a charity letter Check your learning: Writing an answer to a question about persuasive language in a letter	• Worksheet 4a: Purpose and audience • Worksheet 4b: Presentational features on *Panic Room* poster • Worksheet 4c: Writing an evaluation about presentational features • Worksheet 4d: Language features used in a letter • Learning activity: Comparing two climate change websites pages • Learning activity: Comparing two educational web pages • Planning activity: Evaluating a media web page
5: The time and the place	1: Using clues in texts to place them in chronological order 2: Using historical texts and looking for clues to the writer's purpose 3: Using additional historical information about a period to reconsider a writer's purpose 4–5: Looking for clues in advertisements to make decisions about social attitudes 6: Writing one or two paragraphs to explain social attitudes expressed through a text 7: Identifying how a poet reveals ideas about different cultures and place through her writing 8–11: Considering and answering questions on how an understanding of the context of a text might reveal a different meaning Check your learning: Recapping understanding of key terms: social context, historical context and cultural context	• Worksheet 5a: Texts in time • Worksheet 5b: Texts and attitudes 1 • Worksheet 5c: Texts and attitudes 2 • Worksheet 5d: Texts, places and cultures • Analysis activity: Advertising • Analysis activity: Texts from other cultures • Planning activity: Texts in context
6: Creating a story	1-2: Exploring the ways in which writers choose to open their story: through setting the scene and creating characters 3: Making suggestions about the impact of the opening scene on the reader	• Worksheet 6a: Openings • Worksheet 6b: Characters • Worksheet 6c: 'Crash'

Chapter	Student Book activities	kerboodle! resources
	4: Comparing narratives to decide which is more effective 5: Exploring how the writer uses dialogue to develop a narrative 6: Exploring how the writer uses contrast to develop a narrative 7: Paired discussion on how a writer chooses to structure a story to engage the reader 8: Analysing how writers choose to end a narrative Check your learning: Recapping understanding of how writers get and keep their readers attention	● Worksheet 6d: Setting ● Worksheet 6e: Dialogue ● Worksheet 6f: Contrast ● Worksheet 6g: Endings ● Worksheet 6h: A twist in the tale ● Viewpoints activity: Effective novel openings ● Analysis activity: Introducing characters ● Planning activity: Interesting settings
7: Understanding arguments	1: Identifying key points in an article 2: Exploring the use of facts and statistics and the effect these have on the reader 3: Examining the writer's choice of emotive language and the reasons for this 4: Explaining why writers use expert opinions to back up their point of view 5: Group discussion about the writers view point and making a judgement on this Check your learning: Writing a developed answer to explain how the writer uses facts, statistics and expert opinions to back up his argument; explaining the writer's choice of words to influence and persuade the reader	● Worksheet 7a: Identifying key points in the Observer article ● Worksheet 7b: Using emotive language ● Worksheet 7c: Making a judgment about the writer's opinion ● Analysis activity: Arguments and language ● Webquest activity: Reading and planning arguments (facts and opinions) ● Viewpoints activity: Effective arguments
8: Responding to texts	1: Sorting facts and opinions 2: Suggesting how a writer might use facts to support his or her point of view 3: Examining how a review uses facts and opinions and what this suggests about the writer's point of view 4: Examining how writers choose words to influence the reader 5: Analysing words used in a text to identify the writer's point of view 6: Forming your own views and expressing them in a response to a text 7: Writing detailed comments about a text to express a point of view Check your learning: Analysing a text to identify facts and opinions, words chosen and the writer's point of view	● Worksheet 8a: Fact and opinion ● Worksheet 8b: Writer's point of view ● Worksheet 8c: 'The "Bore" Lords' ● Worksheet 8d: Using words to influence the reader ● Worksheet 8e: Recognising the writer's viewpoint ● Learning activity: Fact and opinion ● Viewpoints activity: The writer's influence ● Analysis activity: Identifying the writer's viewpoint
9: Exploring the writer's viewpoint	1–2: Reading two texts and forming first impressions of the writer's thoughts and feelings 3: Using evidence from the text to make suggestions about what it shows about the writer's point of view 4–5: Using the cultural context to find out more about the writer's views 6: Using evidence from the text to interpret what the writer thinks 7–8: Selecting words and phrases from a text to back up the writer's viewpoint Check your learning: Writing an interpretation of a text	● Worksheet 9a: Following clues to the writer's viewpoint 1 ● Worksheet 9b: Following clues to the writer's viewpoint 2 ● Worksheet 9c: Understanding the writer's perspective – Sorrento ● Worksheet 9d: Understanding the writer's perspective – Sousse ● Viewpoints activity: Finding the writer's viewpoint in newspapers ● Analysis activity: Texts form other cultures ● Planning activity: Viewpoints in travel writing
10: Comparing texts	1–3: Using criteria to identify similarities and differences 4: Writing an article comparing two phones, offering opinions on both and focussing on the language used to make comparisons 5–8: Examining features of two poems 9: Identifying similarities and differences between two poems; paired discussion of the similarities and differences and then writing a comparison of two poems Check your learning: Reviewing the learning from the chapter Stretch yourself: Choosing two poems from the *AQA Anthology* and recording similarities and differences between them	● Worksheet 10a: Making a comparison ● Worksheet 10b: Mobile phone advertisements ● Worksheet 10c: The language of comparison ● Worksheet 10d: 'The Thickness of Ice' ● Worksheet 10e: Comparing poems 1 ● Worksheet 10f: Comparing poems 2 ● Analysis activity: Comparing non-fiction texts 1 ● Learning activity: Comparing non-fiction texts 2 ● Planning activity: Comparing poems

Chapter	Student Book activities	kerboodle! resources
11: Making your reading skills count in the exam	1: Making notes on possible answers to sample exam questions and then using a simple mark scheme to check points have been covered 2: Analysing a sample student answer and making suggestions to improve it 3: Writing comments on a sample Question 5; peer assessing another student's comments 4: Paired/group discussion on how to respond to a sample Question 6; then writing a sample response	• Worksheet 11a: Sample questions • Worksheet 11b: Sample answers • Worksheet 11c: Your response • Write and assess activity: Understanding non-fiction texts 1 • On your marks activity: Understanding non-fiction texts 2 • Write and assess activity: Understanding non-fiction texts 3
12: Making your reading skills count in the controlled assessment	1: Reading a poem and looking at the annotations which explain the different techniques used 2: Reading and comparing student responses to a controlled assessment task 3: Giving suggestions for improving a sample answer	• Worksheet 12a: Sample answers • Learning activity: Extended reading on poetry • On your marks activity: Extended reading on 'themes' • Planning activity: Planning an extended reading response

Student checklist worksheet

Read through the following list of skills which you will be expected to show in your Reading work for GCSE English or GCSE English Language.

Rate your own skills using the columns as a tick chart and then check out which chapters might be most suited to help you tackle any areas you are not sure about.

Skill	Very confident	Quite confident	Sometimes I can't	Often I can't	Which chapters might help?
Skim a text					1
Scan a text					1
Use text marking					1
Identify presentational features in a text and how they are used					2, 4
Explain how writers use language to create character, setting and mood					3, 4
Write an evaluation of a text					4
Relate texts to their cultural, social and historical contexts					5
Explain how stories are structured					6
Identify facts and statistics in a text					7, 8
Explain how writers use facts and statistics to make a point					7, 8
Identify opinions in a text					8
Use facts and opinions to work out a writer's point of view					8
Identify the writer's point of view					8, 9
Write detailed comments about a text					3, 9
Use evidence to back up my ideas					9
Express my own views about a text					9
Make comparisons between texts					10

Use your responses to the checklist to set yourself *no more than* three targets to achieve from the Reading section.

1...

2...

3...

Checking students' progress

Tasks that may be suitable for assessing progress through the Reading chapters. In all cases, the mark scheme which will be most appropriate is that supplied by AQA for assessing the component of the qualification.

Chapter	AO focus	Activity from Student Book and learning outcomes
1	Read and understand texts, selecting material appropriate to purpose	**Chapter 1, Check your learning** **Students:** ● identify organisational features in a text ● explain how these features are used – issue a reading text and points made in each paragraph, ask students to text mark or list evidence to support the points.
2–4	Explain and evaluate how writers use linguistic, grammatical, structural and presentational features to achieve effects and engage and influence the reader	**Chapter 4, Activities 4 and 5** **Students:** ● choose a non-fiction text (e.g. advert, article, web page, etc.) ● choose a focus, e.g. how the writer uses linguistic features ● annotate the text – underline the features, comment on the impact of the chosen feature. Model the process. Lots of practice 'makes perfect'.
5	Understand texts in their social, cultural and historical context	**Chapter 5, Activity 10** **Students:** ● write a response based on 'Futility' ● make links to the context in which the poem was written ● include their own personal response to the poem and how it makes them feel. **Practice** ● Issue a text form and explain the social, cultural or historical context. ● Ask students to mark places where the ideas expressed, settings mentioned or language used reflects the context. ● Model how to complete the task. Allow students to complete in pairs and take feedback.
6–9	Develop and sustain interpretation of writer's ideas and perspectives	**Chapter 7, Check your learning** **Students:** ● write developed answers to two questions, using examples from the text to support the points they make ● explain clearly how the writer uses facts, opinions and statistics to support an argument ● explain how the writer uses words to influence and persuade the reader. **Practice** ● Issue a text and a table to students as suggested below. Adjust the aspects to suit the text you have chosen. ● Model how to complete the text. ● Allow students to complete the table. Take feedback. Mark tables to assess progress. {{TABLE2}}

Inner table for chapters 6–9:

Aspect of the text	Main point(s)	Devices used by the writer
Opening paragraph		
Paragraphs 2–4		
Final paragraph		
Is it effective?		

Chapter	AO focus	Activity from Student Book and learning outcomes
		Chapter 9, Check your learning **Students**: • write one paragraph in response to a question • explain how the writer reveals his/her views and the effects the descriptions, words and vocabulary used have on the reader • make links between the opening lines and the rest of the text • refer to details from the text in their answer • write using appropriate vocabulary • include their own interpretation of the text. **Practice** Present students with a non-fiction text. • Ask the students to work in pairs to identify the reader's viewpoint: Perhaps give a range of adjectives to choose from, e.g. angry, amused, irritated, etc. You might choose to start by making a statement – For example: The writer of this text is convinced of the importance of exercise in developing a healthy body and mind. • Ask the students to find five pieces of evidence from the text that reflect his/her viewpoint. Take feedback. • Show the students how to use the evidence to explain the writer's stance. Highlight key vocabulary, e.g. 'this suggests ...' or 'this implies ...' • Ask students to write about two or three of their chosen extracts. Take feedback or peer assess (or do both).
10	Collate and make comparisons and cross-reference as appropriate.	Comparisons are made on objective criteria. For example, poems are compared according to their content, theme, language, structure; advertisements may be compared on the way they use language, pictures/images and colour. **Chapter 10, Activity 9** **Students**: • write five paragraphs comparing two given poems • compare the use of language, structure and presentation in each poem • include their own personal response to the poems • use quotations from the poems to support their points. **Practice** • Issue table with criteria down the side and the headings 'Text 1', 'Text 2' and 'Similarities/Differences' along the top. • Model for students how to fill in the table. • Ask students to complete. • Take oral feedback or mark the table. {table}

Criteria	Text 1	Text 2	Similarities/ Differences
Use of language			
Use of pictures			
Use of colour			

General resources

The resources in the Student Book, Teacher's Book and *kerboodle!* provide a range of learning opportunities for students and give them practice at developing their skills using a wide variety of text types. The resources suggested below can be used to reinforce, develop and extend students' skills and learning further.

General resources	Author and title
Short stories: extracts from the short stories in the *AQA Anthology* may be useful for practise in identifying varied sentences and the effects created.	• Haruki Murakami: 'On Seeing the 100% Perfect Girl One Beautiful Morning' • Elizabeth Baines: 'Compass and Torch' • Penelope Lively: 'The Darkness Out There' • Helen Dunmore: 'My Polish Teacher's Tie' • Clare Wigfall: 'When the Wasps Drowned' • Leila Aboulela: 'Something Old, Something New' • Ridjal Noor: 'Anil'
It's Now or Never: collection of short stories edited by Leggett and Blatchford: published by Bell & Hyman. The stories demonstrate effective beginnings and endings; plot structure and character development; variety of writers' viewpoints; range of themes – social issues, love/romance, relationships and genres, such as science fiction, romance, (civil) war.	• Jennifer Gubb: 'Pin Money' • Paul Theroux: 'White Lies' • Arthur C. Clarke: 'Reunion • R.T Kurosaki: 'A Lot to Learn' • Jane Rogers: 'True Romance' • Patrick O'Brian: 'Samphire' • Liam O'Flaherty: 'The Sniper'
Additional reading: Chatwin, Bryson and Theroux offer differing approaches to the travel-writing genre: extracts will demonstrate viewpoint and tone.	• Bruce Chatwin: *The Songlines* • Bill Bryson: *Notes from a Small Island* • Paul Theroux: *To the Ends of the Earth* • Richard Bach: *Jonathan Livingston Seagull* – fable and homily • *Empire Magazine (or similar)* – exemplars for deconstructing moving image texts through review/comment. • *Here Today* – selected by Ted Hughes A collection of modern poems published by Hutchinson. Arranged thematically, good for looking at form, structure and writer's viewpoint Further suggestions • 'Whatever Happened to Lulu' ⎫ • 'Icarus Allsorts' ⎬ Roger McGough • 'The Identification' ⎭ • 'The Road Not Taken' Robert Frost • 'Sometimes it Happens' Brian Patten ⎫ work well • 'Absence' Elizabeth Jennings ⎬ together • 'Rising Five' from Here Today Norman Nicholson • 'Initial Illumination' Tony Harrison
Useful websites for support materials. The BFI site is good for resources and training for teachers.	• www.poets.org • www.poetryarchive.org • www.guardian.co.uk • www.bfi.org.uk

AO focus

English AO2 Reading and English Language AO3 Studying written language

- Read and understand texts, selecting material appropriate to purpose, collating from different sources.

- Explain and evaluate how writers use presentational features to achieve effects and engage and influence the reader.

In this chapter your students will:

- learn how to text mark a text
- develop their skills in skimming and scanning
- learn how to use presentational clues to help them find information.

Additional resources

Worksheets

1a: Car design

1b: Focus on the positives

1c: Smoke alarms

Getting started

Introduce the purpose of the lesson as learning how to get information from texts. Ask students to explain how they usually gather information from newspapers, magazines or the internet. Invite them to explain any problems they may have in locating information. Read through the objectives and the opening paragraph of Chapter 1 so students know that they will be engaging with texts to improve their skills in this area.

Working through the chapter

In this section, students will learn about marking and annotating texts in order to make it easier to locate information. This may be a revision exercise for some, but others may need support to be able to become successful readers of non-fiction texts.

Text marking

Read through the explanation of what text marking involves and check that students understand it is more than just highlighting sections. Focus attention on the need to address the question and so find the pertinent information. Look at the worked example on Judo (Text A) and the annotated comments which the student makes on the text. Ask students to think about how the annotations help to answer the question as well as the chosen phrases. Look at the need to read 'into' the text, that is, to think about what the writer *means*. Use the example of 'For those who are competitive ...'. Invite students to explain how that links with the idea of winning things as the annotation indicates.

Activity 1 Students may be provided with Worksheet 1a, which contains Text B, to carry out this activity.

a Using Text A as an example, students should be directed to identify points which answer the question posed. If they are using the worksheet, students could use pens and annotate directly onto the text; otherwise they should locate the relevant details and copy them out. If copying the text out, students should try to explain the quotes in their own words. Remind students that, to answer the question, they need to be able to show understanding of the comments and not just be able to pick out suitable passages.

Students may select details such as:

- The shape of a car can help airflow so it can go faster.
- Cars have rounded shapes to make the air flow better.
- Some cars have parts that direct air underneath a car.
- Some cars have a spoiler (or rear-wing) to stop the car being lifted by air.

b Sharing ideas with other students should help to establish that there may be a range of correct answers in the text, but that individuals will select them in different ways. It may be suitable to share results round the group.

Skimming and scanning

🔘 Learning activity: Skimming and scanning a website

🔘 Learning activity: Identifying text types

Students sometimes find these two concepts quite difficult to distinguish between, so it may be useful to compare these reading skills by suggesting two images. 'Skimming stones' is a game played on water where the object is to get a pebble to touch the surface at a number of points as it moves across the water. 'Skim reading' is similar in that you just drop on certain points looking for key words and phrases so the whole text does not have to be read. 'Scanning' suggests the idea of looking quite carefully across an area to identify particular things, like being on a beach and scanning the horizon for ships. When reading, to scan a text is to do the same, look for points or words in a particular section of text. Link these images with the definitions in the Key terms feature box.

Skimming

Read through the paragraph about Newcastle (Text C). Draw attention to the way the opening sentence indicates what the remainder of the paragraph will contain. Ask students to identify which word in the first sentence best suggests what the rest is about. Direct them then to 'skim' the paragraph and pick out names of the landmarks in Newcastle. Less confident readers may need to be reminded that names of places start with capital letters, so when skimming for particular names, they should look primarily for words that begin with a capital. Invite students to locate three place names as quickly as possible. Caution that words which start a sentence and which also start with a capital letter will not be acceptable answers!

Activity 2 This activity uses Text D.

This independent activity is intended to consolidate the skimming skill practised on the Newcastle text. Time students for the suggested one minute as they read through Text D, which is about Comic Relief. Students who are entitled to a reader as part of their Access Arrangements may require slightly longer, or may need the text to be read aloud.

Discuss which answer from **Paragraph 1** is correct. The correct answer is:

ii   It gives a brief description of what takes place on Red Nose Day.

The other two are incorrect because:

i   The work is mentioned only towards the end, the main focus is the activities that day.

iii   There is no mention of the reader giving money after reading it.

In **Paragraph 2**, the correct answer is:

ii   It encourages the reader to donate to Comic Relief.

This is a harder question as it needs the student to infer the answer from reading about how the money is used and what others do to support the events.

Scanning

Remind students of the purpose of scanning and the text marking activity they carried out at the start, as both of these will be useful skills to use for the next activity.

Activity 3 This activity uses Text E.

This is a reinforcement activity for students to practise their skills in identifying information relevant to answering questions. The questions require students to locate particular information quickly from Text E. Direct students to look for the word in bold in the activity first and then pick out the information necessary to answer the question. You may wish to distinguish between this task and the skimming task by referring students to look quickly over the whole text to find key words. You could model locating the word 'stars' so students understand what to do. Narrating your search will assist students even more – perhaps along the lines of 'I need to find the answer to the question about how many stars the hotel has. I'm looking across the first line to see if I can spot the word "star". When I find it I stop to pick out how many stars are mentioned – three. So I have the answer'. Encourage students to do the same sort of thing for the subsequent questions with a teaching assistant if available, or with another student to give more confidence in their own abilities to do this.

The second part of the activity (f to i) asks the students to identify the key words themselves and then locate the answers.

Answers	
a	Train
b	By tram
c	The coastline of Lancashire and the countryside
d	Nico
e	Yes
f	North
g	Ambleside
h	Preston and Lancaster

Students may use Worksheet 1b for skimming and scanning practice.

Signposts

k! Planning activity: Researching obesity

This section will expand students' understanding of the other techniques that writers use to assist their readers in locating information. Check that students understand what is meant by 'subheadings', 'bullet points' and 'bold print'. The information in the Student Book provides clear examples of how each of these are used to enable a reader to find information. If you wish to provide actual examples, you may want to use the part of this chapter already covered and pick out ways that the writers of this section have used similar devices to structure the text and let students know what they are learning about. For example, the texts 'Car Design' and 'Newcastle' have used both a subheading and bold font to draw attention, plus the Objectives box at the start uses bullet points to quickly inform about learning targets for the chapter.

Activity 4 This activity uses Text F.

The question directs students to use the organisational devices to find the correct answers in Text F. Ensure students understand that these are the devices outlined above.

Students should read the text and questions carefully and use the devices to assist them in finding the following answers.

Answers	
a	One per floor.
b	Place the alarm on a ceiling, Near or at the middle of the room, 30 cm from a wall or light.
c	One that lasts longest.
d	To alert people in the house to the danger of fire, giving time to escape.
e	A range of possible answers include: place it correctly so it can be heard; change the batteries annually; test it once a week by pressing the test button; replace the whole unit every ten years.
f	Bottom of the staircase.

Plenary

Check your learning It may be helpful for students to use Worksheet 1c: Smoke alarms (Text F). If this is not available, students should be directed to record their answers to the questions.

Encourage students to answer the questions independently as they will need to do in the exam. Remind students to use the skills they have been working on during this chapter:

- text marking (perhaps with annotations)
- skimming
- scanning
- using presentational features.

Peer assessment may be useful for checking responses and comparing ideas.

Ask students to sum up in a sentence what they have learnt about how to find information from the chapter. It may also be suitable to discuss which aspect of the Personal Learning and Thinking Skills have been utilised to enable them to be successful – answers may include Team workers (if they have worked successfully in a group) and Reflective learners (if they have had the chance to review their knowledge and act on the outcomes).

Outcomes

In this chapter your students have:

- improved their ability to extract information from texts using a range of strategies
- learned how to use text marking to identify relevant points
- understood skimming and scanning purposes and strategies
- learned how to use presentational features to identify key points.

2 Making an impact

AO focus

**English AO2 Reading and English Language
AO3 Studying written language**

- Read and understand texts, selecting material appropriate to purpose, collating from different sources.
- Explain and evaluate how writers use presentational features to achieve effects and engage and influence the reader.

In this chapter your students will:

- examine how texts are organised
- think about how texts are presented to attract and influence the reader.

Additional resources

Worksheets

2a: Purposes and audiences of the front cover

2b: Use of pictures and colours

2c: Use of words and fonts

2d: Writing about features 1

2e: Writing about features 2

Getting started

If possible, before the start of the lesson you may wish to write the words 'purpose' and 'audience' on the board. Introduce the lesson focus by looking at the objectives in the Student Book. Link these with the expectations that students will have to comment on organisation and presentation for the reading section of the exam.

Purpose and audience

 Connecting comments activity: Analysing a web page

In this section students will learn about how writers write for specific purposes and audiences and understand that texts may have more than one purpose and audience.

Before reading the section in the Student Book, give students two minutes to work in pairs and produce definitions for the word on the board and then take ideas about their meanings. Encourage discussion about different purposes and audiences. If suitable, suggest/show several

different texts: a label from a can; a magazine advert; a newspaper article and invite students to suggest possible purposes and audiences and provide the reasons for their suggestions. Compare the ideas from the students with the explanations printed in the Student Book which focuses on the front page of the leaflet for *An Inspector Calls* (Text A). Students may need an explanation about the roles of a writer and graphic designer. It is important that they understand that the 'writer' refers to the person who has written the text for the leaflet, not the writer of the play.

Working through the chapter

Move on to looking at Text A in more detail. Students should read through the list of suggested purposes for design of the front cover.

Activities 1 and 2 Both activities use the front page of the *An Inspector Calls* leaflet (Text A).

Activity 1 uses the 'purposes' table.

It may be useful for Worksheet 2a to be used to assist with recording responses to the first activity on purposes and also the second activity on identification of audiences.

a The 'Purpose' column on the table should be completed using the bulleted list on page 9. More able students may be able to suggest other purposes, which should be included on their table, providing they are able to justify their ideas with an example based on the text.

b Students may need to be encouraged to think about appropriateness of subject matter suggested by the leaflet and also the type of play that is being suggested by the poster (Text A). Look at the cartoon illustration and invite students to link the characters with an audience type from the list. Remind students of the list of purposes they have already included in the first table, which the leaflet is intended to address when they consider who the likely audiences may be. They could move on from that point to consider the other audience groups and record their ideas on the worksheet.

A mini-plenary at this point may be useful to check that students have understood the activities that have already been done through looking at the leaflet. Discussion of some of the ideas given should identify any students who may require further clarification.

Form and features

(k) Learning activity: Analysing a website

The following section is intended to assist students to learn about the different choices that writers of texts make about the appearance of the text and the ways that images and colours can be used to provide messages to a reader.

Students should read the section about form and features. You may wish to check their understanding of what form and features mean before moving on to the activities associated with the concepts.

Form: the way writing is organised and structured on the page.

Features: the ways that text can be presented: colours, font style and size.

Pictures and colours

Students who are visual learners may be assisted by having a range of different items to look at while discussing this topic. Select images on advertisements, perhaps from popular magazines and invite students to respond to the way colour and pictures are used to convey messages about the products being advertised. Discuss what the advertisement is trying to do and who is expected to respond to it; you could link this with the opening activity of the chapter. This could then be linked with the task in the Student Book looking at a similar choice about pictures and colours.

It may be useful to check the students' understanding of 'Atmosphere/mood' before beginning the activity which focuses on the use of colour and images. Students who experience difficulties with responding to inference may need support to identify the aspects being shown by the images and assistance to explain the ways colour is being used.

Activity 3 This activity uses the 'Use of images and colour' table and the front page of the *An Inspector Calls* leaflet (Text A).

Worksheet 2b may be appropriate for recording responses to the pictures and colours for this activity. Support may be usefully provided to students who find 'reading' images difficult. The 'Prompts' may need further explanation before an answer is appropriate.

Words and fonts

Read through the section in the Student Book. It may be useful to look at the illustration which demonstrates the impact that font size can have on attracting an audience. Discuss ways that students have observed this in operation, for example, in supermarkets, hoardings, etc. Alternatively, show examples of different sized fonts/colours which feature the same words (for example, For Sale; Free!; Fire Exit) and ask students to respond to the ways they are presented. Link these observations with the following activity which asks students to comment on the leaflet and its use of words and text style.

Activity 4 This activity uses the 'Use of words and text styles' table and the front page of the *An Inspector Calls* leaflet (Text A).

Worksheet 2c may be suitable to record responses to this activity.

a Students should respond to the ways that the words are chosen for effect on a reader. Some of the prompts may need additional explanation for students who find inferential reading difficult. The second part of the table expects students to focus on how the words are presented, not what they are saying. Refer back to the earlier activity where different words using different fonts were discussed and link the comments made then about impact with the task to be done on the leaflet.

b and c Sharing ideas should expand students' understanding of how the words and styles have been used. Encourage students to add further details that they had not considered, as the task is intended to draw a wide response, not a 'right' one.

Writing about features

(k) Planning activity: Analysing an electronic text

This section draws the previous ideas together and shows students how to write about text. It may be useful for students to have the worksheets they have completed or the copied details available to refer to.

Students should read the information outlining how to write about impact and effect. Ask students to revise the meanings of 'impact', 'feature' and 'effect' by reading the Key terms feature box. Share the reading of the highlighted text. Discuss the comments made by the writer in response to the chosen features. Check students' understanding of this skill by asking the group to select another aspect of the colours used and commenting on their use in the same way.

Activity 5 This activity uses the front page of the *An Inspector Calls* leaflet (Text A) and a student's response (Text C).

Students could use Worksheet 2d to highlight the next section of the response and also to continue with their own paragraph. If copying the text from the Student Book, suggest that this is done before trying to select features and write the explanation of how these have been used.

Activity 6 This activity uses the table from Activity 4 to analyse word and fonts in Text A.

a Using the model text and the completed tasks from the section on 'Words and fonts', students should try writing their own response to those aspects of the leaflet. They should also suggest reasons why the particular words and fonts have been chosen. Remind students that this will need to be in sentences as seen in the example.

b Sharing the activity where different sections are highlighted should help students see their response from another's point of view. This may assist with refining ideas and checking that there are explanations given as well as features identified.

c Some students find it difficult to accept constructive criticism and may be averse to admitting there are areas that could be improved. Suggest that this could be restricted to a single point from each student. More able students may wish to carry out edits and improvements. This may be a suitable independent task or homework.

These could be shared with peers to assist in improving skills as both writers and readers.

Check your learning This activity uses the centre pages of *An Inspector Calls* leaflet (Text D).

Students should read through the middle section of the leaflet independently, using the skills they have developed over the chapter. It may be useful for students to refer to the worksheets used if they need to recap on which features

they have commented upon already and how they did this.

Students who experience difficulties with inferential reading may benefit from being guided to focus on each feature in turn and then carry out the task associated with it. More able students may prefer to write a more 'blended' response dealing with the text as a whole rather than breaking it into the suggested component parts.

Plenary

Invite students to share their responses to Text A with the group and invite others to comment on the ways that they have selected and explained the features.

Refer to the objectives of the chapter and check whether students feel they have achieved the stated aim of the session. Remind students that by completing the tasks in this chapter they have been acting as independent enquirers and also team workers. Invite students to give examples of what they have done that fits into these categories. Discuss responses and consider any views that suggest other Personal Learning and Thinking Skills have also been addressed in part.

Outcomes

In this chapter your students have:

- read and responded to texts
- commented on features of texts
- shared ideas about presentation of texts
- written about how the reader is affected by presentational devices
- recorded ideas about effects
- peer assessed work.

AO focus

English AO2 Reading and English Language AO3 Studying written language

- Read and understand texts, selecting material appropriate to purpose, collating from different sources.

- Explain and evaluate how writers use structure and presentational features to achieve effects and engage and influence the reader.

In this chapter your students will:

- read a variety of texts
- examine how writers use words to create character, setting and mood
- learn how to develop comments on details in a text.

Additional resources

Worksheets

3a: Characters 1

3b: Characters 2

3c: *Oliver Twist*

3d: Response to a short story opening

3e: 'The Park Hotel'

Getting started

Introduce the objectives for the session from the Student Book. Ensure students understand that this reading section is preparation for the controlled assessment for their GCSE qualification, so it is important for them to be confident about working on tasks independently. Read through the opening paragraph of the chapter and ensure students understand that they will be responding to various texts to evaluate the way writers use words to affect readers. It will also be necessary for them to understand the terms outlined in the Key terms feature box.

Working through the chapter

Characters

[kt] Planning activity: Creating characters

[kt] Viewpoints activity: *On My Own Two Feet*

In this section students read about a character and consider how description provides a reader with clues about his personality.

Introduce this section by asking students to consider characters they know from films or TV programmes. For students who are visual learners it may be useful to provide students with a selection of images of characters from well-known/popular programmes or recent films and ask for brief explanations about each one. Invite responses to how these characters behave or speak and the audience reaction to what they can see. Draw out that some characters are clearly intended to be 'bad' or 'good'. Link this with the way that the writer of film/TV script has created them to be that way and that characters in stories are also created with a purpose in mind.

Direct students to read the first extract about Seth Thompson and look at the annotations to help students identify the ways the writer builds up an image of what he is like. Draw attention to the various devices being used.

Activity 1   This activity uses 'Seth Thompson' (Text A), and Worksheet 3a.

a   Worksheet 3a may be useful for students to record their responses to the character. It may be helpful for students to use coloured pens or highlighters to assist with picking out relevant details.

b   Personal response to the characters in a text is an important part of reading. Encourage students to use Standard English to explain their views of the character based on what has been read. Ensure students know that they can only base their views on the text provided, not their own speculation about what sort of a person he may be. Give students the opportunity to share their responses and invite them to justify their views by referring to the text extract for suitable quotes. Compare views and discuss how or why students may have differing opinions. Encourage students to understand that others may not share their views of a character as they have focused on different parts of their behaviour, but this is acceptable providing it can be justified.

Dialogue

In this section, students use a script extract to piece together an impression of characters based solely on how each one speaks.

Activity 2   This activity uses an extract from the play *Blood Brothers* by Willy Russell (Text C).

Students would probably benefit from working in pairs on the next section as it will allow them to read the script extract in a more dramatic way. Ensure that students read the background information and understand that the writer has made the characters speak differently on purpose to create particular effects in the audience.

Before reading, you may wish to check that your students understand they need to make notes about the characters based on what each one says and how they say it. This could be done by reading the text twice and picking out relevant details the second time around. The recording of information about each character based on what they read could also be carried out as a paired activity.

Following the reading, students should read the commentary (Text D) below it. It may be useful to share this short text with the whole group in order to check that students understand the way to use quotes and points to support their ideas.

Activity 3 This activity also uses Text C.

Students should be encouraged to work independently when they are writing about the way Mickey speaks. It may be useful to provide students who experience writing difficulties with the writing frame on Worksheet 3b. Encourage students to share their ideas about Mickey with their partner. More able students could use quotes to support their points in the discussion.

A mini-plenary at this point may assist students in understanding that different readers may respond in different ways to text, so sharing of ideas and comments with the whole group may be useful. Use both the texts already studied to draw out points about character and how the writer influences readers.

Setting

Analysis activity: Setting the scene

This section provides students with opportunities to learn how writers use feelings about places and description to affect the reader's response to a setting. When introducing this section, it may be useful to show a series of images of different locations and take responses to them from students. Invite them to consider how they might feel if they were visiting the place, living there, lost there etc. Encourage students to see that depending on the situation, an individual could feel quite differently about locations. Link this with the introductory text in the Student Book which focuses on settings.

Activity 4 Students should read through an extract from *Nicholas Nickleby* by Charles Dickens (Text E).

a Students should be encouraged to share their selected features and respond to what is being described.

b Students will hopefully identify that the last choice in the bullet points is the correct answer. Encourage use of their selected details to help with any students who are uncertain about which is the correct response.

Following on from the earlier work using images, it may assist students to attempt to produce a rough drawing of the scene. This may help them to focus on the highlighted sections but will also improve the understanding of visual learners when imagining the scene. The commentary could be used as annotations for their drawing. Students should read the comments (Text F) written by a student in the Student Book. It may be appropriate to discuss with the group how far they agree with what the student has written. Invite students to write a further sentence about the extract using one of the six items they selected in a) and making a comment about what it shows about the school. Ideas could be shared to see the range of responses that students have.

Activity 5 This activity uses an extract from *Oliver Twist* by Charles Dickens (Text G). This is also available on Worksheet 3c and can be used for annotation and highlighting purposes.

a You may wish to focus attention on the two aspects outlined, the sights and sounds of the market place. Students should try to identify at least two examples for each bullet point.

b The word 'reeking' may be unfamiliar to students. Though likely to make a guess at the meaning based on context it may be helpful to offer students the chance to use dictionaries.

c Students should be encouraged to prepare their ideas by writing notes etc. before beginning to write a commentary on how Dickens has described the sounds of the market morning. Students may wish to use dictionaries to check the meanings of words which are unfamiliar to them, though it needs to be understood that this will not be an option in the controlled assessment.

Students may benefit from being able to share their ideas with more than one other student, perhaps by joining two pairs to compare responses. Encourage students to share what they have learnt about the way the text is written and any word meanings they have found out. Invite students who have used dictionaries to demonstrate their understanding by using the word in another sentence so others can also learn how to use it.

Creating mood

Students may be familiar with the idea of 'mood' from the previous chapter. In this section they will learn how writers try to provoke an emotional response in readers by the way they choose to write. It may assist students to understand this technique through using music taken from film soundtracks, such as 'Jaws', 'Psycho' or 'The Exorcist'. These may provide some auditory clues about mood and atmosphere even if students are unfamiliar with the film itself.

Students should read through the introductory paragraph of the story (Text H). Remind them about the techniques already used to pick out how writers have used details for particular effects.

Activity 6 This activity uses Worksheet 3d, which may enable students to record their responses to the text.

a Support may be offered to students who find inferential reading difficult.

b–c Some students may also need reminders about what an 'adjective' is and some assistance with identifying them in the text before being able to replace them.

d Sharing their results will assist students in understanding that there are alternate ways to address a task and those different results may be equally correct.

The final text is a non-fiction extract (Text I), but students need to be made aware that this type of writing uses similar devices to fiction writing. Focus attention on the clues given in the opening comments about how the text is made to be 'appealing'. By this point, it may be appropriate to encourage students to work independently on the final activity in order to consolidate skills and build up confidence in their own abilities.

Creating a tone

This section deals with the way a writer can choose to convey an attitude through the words chosen. The student is shown how this is intended to have a specific effect on a reader.

Activity 7 This activity uses 'The Park Hotel' (Text I).

Some students who experience difficulties with reading may prefer to work with support from a peer or teaching assistant to complete the activity. Worksheet 3e may support students in their responses to the questions. Remind students that it is necessary to comment on the points they

choose as they have done with the other texts in this chapter.

a Students should record their responses either on the worksheet or elsewhere. Remind them that the focus is on how the place is made to sound appealing.

b Though being instructed to carry out a counting task, students are required to understand the notion of 'addressing the reader directly'. Check that students realise this means use of the second person in the text. Students should be able to see that this makes the text appeal to the reader as if they are important, make it sound more personal and engages their interest more.

c The task of changing some words to alter the tone may be difficult for students who are not confident readers. It may be helpful to provide a number of alternate words which convey another tone for students to use, for example, boring, uncomfortable, dirty, untidy.

Plenary

Check your learning Direct students to the final section 'Check your learning' and allow three minutes for paired discussion about the two points suggested. Invite students to feed back in their pairs what they have learnt about these aspects. Take feedback from the whole group to create a whole class list of the five main learning points from this chapter. Then you could discuss if any Personal Learning and Thinking Skills have been addressed through the work done and take suggestions about which ones have been covered and in which ways students think this has been done.

Outcomes

In this chapter your students have:

- read and responded to fiction and non-fiction texts
- commented on the effects of texts
- shared ideas about characters, settings and language
- written about how the reader is affected by word and phrase choice
- recorded ideas about effects
- peer assessed work.

4 Evaluating texts

AO focus

English AO2 Reading and English language AO3 Studying written language

- Read and understand texts, selecting material appropriate to purpose, collating from different sources.
- Explain and evaluate how writers use linguistic, structural and presentational features to achieve effects and engage and influence the reader.

In this chapter your students will:

- build on what they have learnt in Chapters 2 and 3
- think about the effectiveness of features of presentation and language
- learn about evaluation
- write an evaluation.

Additional resources

Worksheets

4a: Purpose and audience

4b: Presentation features on *Panic Room* poster

4c: Writing an evaluation about presentational features

4d: Language features used in a letter

Getting started

It would be advisable to work through this chapter after completion of work on Chapters 2 and 3, as the work in Chapter 4 builds on the work done in those sections. This is highlighted in the objectives panel of the Student Book.

Introduce the other objectives. Students may already have an understanding of the term 'evaluate' which they have learnt in other subject areas. It may be useful to encourage cross-curricular understanding and transfer of skills by asking students to explain how they have used evaluation as a tool in other areas (for example, technology). It may be useful to encourage recall of the meaning of 'audience', 'purpose' and 'presentational features' before students read through the introductory paragraph about evaluation as these are words they have already been taught in the earlier chapters. Direct students to use the Key terms feature box if they need further reminders about some of the terms being used in this section.

Working through the chapter

Purpose and audience

 Learning activity: Comparing two climate change websites

In this section, students will revise their knowledge about the reasons texts may be written and who they may be written for.

Students may find it useful to have some examples of different texts to look at before going on to Activity 1. It may be possible to provide examples of the types of texts suggested which may assist weaker students with working out the intended audience and purposes. This could be on interactive whiteboard. Kinaesthetic learners may also find it beneficial to be able to handle actual examples. If this is not possible, encourage students to use examples of text that can be seen in the room to suggest intended audiences and purposes (for example, a sports club notice, or an evacuation procedures sign).

Activity 1 Worksheet 4a may support the recording of responses to the texts.

Students should be encouraged to discuss their ideas to widen their views and assist them in understanding that texts may have more than one purpose and audience. Check students have correctly identified appropriate audiences and purposes by inviting feedback from the group before moving on.

Presentation and language

 Planning activity: Comparing two educational websites

This section draws in part on the work done in earlier chapters, and also extends students' understanding of the range of presentational features that they may come across. They learn how to apply this knowledge to texts and justify their responses. It may be useful to remind students about work done previously on aspects of this topic. References to the previous two chapters may assist students in recalling work already done.

Activity 2 This activity uses a spread from a fairytale book for children (Text A) and The Phenon laptop computer advert (Text B).

Students should be directed to use the bulleted lists of features to match with the images and text shown. Check that students understand what each one means and can locate suitable examples in the texts provided.

Activity 3 Encourage pairs to share ideas about intended purpose and audience of each text and amend their results as necessary. Discussion about the suitability of the presentational features could be expanded to the whole group.

Stretch yourself

Encourage more able students to expand their understanding of this area, by providing another text from an entirely different genre for them to use in a similar exercise. Invite them to identify a range of features and the purpose and audience for the text.

Evaluation: making a judgement

In this section students will make comments on a media text based on their opinions. It will also extend their understanding of how purpose and audience are targeted.

The main teaching point in the introductory text is that evaluation is a matter of opinion, so students need to understand that there is no right or wrong response – providing they can give reasons for what they think. To demonstrate this, it may be useful to write a series of four to five statements on cards/paper which can be distributed randomly to students. Ask individuals to read 'their' statement out and then give their opinion on it (i.e. do they agree or not), with a reason explaining their view. For example, 'Science is the best subject to learn' or 'My most important possession is my phone'. Invite other students to say whether they feel sufficient reason has been given to back up the opinion being offered. Link this activity with the Student Book section which could be read afterwards.

Activity 4

Planning activity: Evaluating a web page

This activity uses the *Panic Room* film poster (Text C).

Worksheet 4b may assist with recording student responses for this activity.

Students should use the poster from *Panic Room* to complete the table about presentational features. Remind them that they need to support their comments with evidence from the poster. Support may be offered via customisation of the worksheet to provide weaker students with some ideas in the 'presentational features' column which they may then use to identify answers in the other columns.

Writing an evaluation about presentational features

This type of activity is similar to the type of task that may appear on exam papers. Students will learn how to write comments about a media text and consider how a sample answer meets marking criteria.

Students should focus on the question being posed. At this point they are not invited to actually write the answer, but think about how they would do so using information they have noted already. It may be helpful to link the question with the exam in which they will need to address similar questions.

The student response (Text D) shown with highlights should be read with the annotations so students can see the features that are noted when marking is done. Invite questions about any aspect of this as students may be unaware of the type of annotations that have to be done on work they submit.

Activity 5 This activity uses the student evaluation of the poster (Text E).

Worksheet 4c has the full text to be used with this task.

This invites students to act as the teacher and mark up text in order to identify and 'reward' the next section of the student response. Students with reading difficulties may need support to identify features successfully and it may be suitable to suggest that perhaps identifying only five or six of the features would be acceptable. It may be appropriate to discuss, as a group, the responses to the text that students have highlighted themselves. Alternatively, pairs could share their ideas with another pair in order to assess how successful their peers have been. More able students could be invited to try and write their own commentary on the same poster, having read a 'model' example.

Stretch yourself

As a useful Stretch yourself activity, students could be shown different posters from a similar genre and invited to write an analysis of the presentational features in one they choose.

Writing an evaluation about language

In this section students apply their knowledge to a written text. They learn about devices that texts may use and identify them in a charity letter.

Students may need reassurance that the skills they have been developing work equally well when looking at language rather than images. The text provided contains examples of a range of features. It might help students see they can use their skills by looking at individual annotations and asking students to find other examples of the features highlighted and then suggesting the effect that these words or phrases are intended to have. For example, use of the personal pronoun 'you' is highlighted, but students may also identify that 'our' and 'we' are also used, which helps the reader to feel involved with the work being described.

Activity 6 This activity uses the letter from a charity (Text F).

Worksheet 4d can be used to support this activity.

This is a similar task to the one students have already done in identifying features on the poster. Check that all the terms being used are understood and can be explained before inviting students to use Worksheet 4d. The notes made for this activity can be used for the final section of the chapter. Support may be provided for students who lack confidence in this type of activity by taking each feature in turn and focusing attention on just finding that one. Alternatively, provide students with a reduced list of items to locate, with the focus being on those that are the least inferential and most explicit. For example, rule of three, use of first person, rhetorical question and facts.

Plenary

Check your learning Direct students to answer the questions in this section independently paying close attention to the bulleted points. Recap on the learning objectives for the lesson. Invite students to pick one thing they have learned about each of the bulleted points and share that with the group. It may be a useful *aide memoir* to create class posters or visuals to display so that there is a constant reminder of what has been learned.

Ask students to identify what they have done in this chapter that fulfils any parts of the Personal Learning and Thinking Skills. Check whether other students agree or can extend the suggestions made.

Stretch yourself
This is an optional activity for more able students.

Some students may benefit from attempting the writing of the final response independently, as this is how they will have to work in the exam. Using the student answer from the previous section as a model may be helpful to students. Encourage use of the notes made, though students need to ensure their ideas are organised appropriately and written in sentences and paragraphs.

Sharing of responses and ideas at the end of the session may help to consolidate skills developed over the course of the chapter and also provide some peer support for students who may have found the final task difficult.

Outcomes

In this chapter your students have:

- read and responded to a range of texts
- identified the audience and purpose for a range of texts
- commented on presentational features of texts
- commented on language features of texts
- responded to images
- considered aspects of marking criteria applied to student responses.

AO focus

English AO2 Reading

Understand texts in their social, cultural and historical context.

In this chapter your students will learn how:

- texts are often shaped by the time in history when they were written
- the culture or the kind of society in which the writer lives can affect what they write.

Additional resources

Worksheets

5a: Texts in time

5b: Texts and attitudes 1

5c: Texts and attitudes 2

5d: Texts, places and cultures

Getting started

Texts in time

Activity 1 The extracts are intended to make it obvious to students that language, its use, its presentation and the way it represents the writer's viewpoint, changes over time. They show how vocabulary and word order have moved from the Middle English of Chaucer to the Modern English of Alan Bennett.

Students might spend a few minutes comparing and discussing the differences and sharing their ideas across the class.

Answers			
	Century/period	Writer	Text
a	16th century	Christopher Marlowe	*Doctor Faustus*
b	20th century	Alan Bennett	*A Woman of No Importance*
c	14th century	Geoffrey Chaucer	*The Knight's Tale*
d	19th century	Oscar Wilde	*The Importance of Being Earnest*

The correct order is: c, a, d, b.

A secondary activity may be to ask the students to look at the extracts where someone is speaking (b and d) and discuss what their words might suggest about their characters.

Issues to consider:

In Extract b repetition of the words, 'I was all right', suggests the speaker is concerned about his/her health. Everything seems to have been fine until Wednesday afternoon when 'all my nice little routine went out the window' and his/her health took a turn for the worse.

In Extract d, the language used is very precise/correct which suggests someone from a good social background. Use of the pronoun 'one' rather than the more usual 'you' reinforces this impression.

Working through the chapter

Activity 2 This activity uses Text A, an extract from *Oliver Twist* by Charles Dickens.

The aim of this activity is to help students appreciate that it can be difficult to understand a text if it is read in a 'vacuum', without some of way of connecting it with the writer's purpose and the things that influenced his/her viewpoint.

Activity 3 This activity uses Text B.

This activity provides additional material to give students something on which to base an understanding of Dickens's purpose. Allow students a few minutes to discuss what they now know and how it can inform their understanding. Review this by drawing ideas from across the class. It may be helpful to reinforce the idea that their impressions need to be rooted in and referenced to the information within the text.

Texts and attitudes

Analysis activity: Advertising

Activity 4 This activity uses the Listerine advert (Text C), and Worksheet 5b.

This activity is intended to help students understand how the images and the text place the advertisement in a specific time and that it reflects the social attitudes of that time. To help them respond to the questions it may be helpful to ask students to look at the image and compare/contrast the representations present there of that period with those of today. Encourage the students to respond as part of a group discussion. This should only take about five minutes including initial looking and thinking time.

Possible answers		
a	i	The woman (Janice) is dressed formally in a bridesmaid dress, her hair has been carefully styled and she is wearing make-up. She appears to have made an effort to look elegant and attractive. The reason for this may be because she is trying to impress single men who may be at the wedding.
	ii	The woman appears to be lonely and a bit sad. There are several indications of this: she is standing at the edge of a room pressed again a curtain and beside a plant in a tall vase, she is standing on her own at a wedding, her facial expression looks sad, her eyes are cast down and she is looking away from the room and out of a window. She is presented as attractive so the viewer wonders why she is alone.
b	i	• Single women looking for romance, a man and potentially a husband • The text in the advert explains that men who initially seem serious about Janice generally lose interest in her. This is linked with the idea of her having bad breath and that being 'a roadblock to romance'.
	ii	**'She's popular with the girls …'** – This seems to imply that whilst Janice is popular with the girls she is not popular with the boys (because she doesn't use Listerine). **'… attractive to men for** *a while*.**'** – This suggests that whilst men are initially interested in her they quickly lose interest (because she doesn't use Listerine). **'Men seem serious – then just courteous – finally, oblivious.'** – This reinforces the previous sentence and implies that men losing interest in her has happened several times previously (because she doesn't use Listerine). **'Halitosis is a roadblock to romance … you're never aware that you're offending!'** – The implication is clear, because she doesn't use Listerine she has bad breath and that is a deterrent to men. She won't get a man until she uses Listerine. This also indicates that all women should use Listerine regardless of whether they know they have bad breath because they don't know that they are offending.
c		**Role of women:** • They need a man. • Getting a man can be competitive so they need to make sure they present themselves perfectly in looks and in smell to catch their man. • Don't want to be left out.

The last aspect of part c) of Activity 4 asks for the students to give their opinion. Allow students time to consider their viewpoint and opportunity to express it. Make sure they include quotes and details from the advertisement to support their opinion.

Activity 5 This activity uses the Suzuki advert (Text D), and Worksheet 5c.

The activity is intended to reinforce the notion of change over time. It may be useful to ask students to consider how the representation in this advertisement picks up on some of the ideas they had in the 'starter' from the previous activity.

Answers	
a	The camera shot shows her as powerful, assertive and confident.
b	Her clothes and pose (her confident strut) show that she is relaxed, in control and that she dresses to please herself.
c	The building: this could be an apartment block (or possibly an office) which shows that she is an independent woman.
d	The words reinforce the women's confidence; the word 'carry' could refer to the way she walks or to the fact she chooses an Ignis to carry her about. The advert suggests that young women in the early part of the 21st century are confident, independent, assertive and that they make their own choices.

Activity 6 The purpose behind this activity is to show students how they can start to build up a developed response to a question. They will draw on their learning from the previous activities in order to demonstrate their understanding of the issues in deconstructing a piece of text and how to express that understanding.

In this activity Text E provides the model for the process students should go through in preparing a written response. That is:

• What are the key points I need to make in this response?

• What is the evidence I will use to support the key points?

• What is the key language I need to use to make the response an effective piece of writing?

Texts, places and cultures

Analysis activity: Texts from other cultures

Activity 7 This activity uses Text F, 'Island Man' by Grace Nichols, and Worksheet 5d.

It provides an opportunity for students to see how writers select language which reflects their viewpoint and purpose. In this case, the writer is drawing upon her own cultural heritage and using it to represent the feelings of a man living away from his place of birth.

Answers	
a	He thinks about: blue surf, wild seabirds, fishermen, the sun.
b	It is an idyllic desert island.
c	'Wombing': womb represents our beginning/birth. It is the thing that gives us life.
d	'Emerald': a precious stone; something of great value.
e	Return to reality begins at line 11 – completed at line 12.
f	London is 'grey' (and) 'metallic'; noisy with 'the surge of wheels' and the 'dull North Circular roar'.

Answers	
g	Last four lines: • 'muffling muffling' suggests stifling/deadening/covering up • 'heaves' suggests reluctance/lack of enthusiasm • 'Another (London day)' suggests repetition/routine/nothing changes • These reinforce the images from **f** to suggest that London does not compare favourably with his homeland.
h	The man is not an individual – he represents all such men (and women) who are away from and miss their place of origin.

Texts in context

Planning activity: Texts in context

Activity 8 This activity uses Text G, 'Futility' by Wilfred Owen.

Before your students start to answer the questions in this activity, it may be useful for them, in pairs, to try reading the poem in different ways to reflect the tone or atmosphere that the poet is aiming for. You could check their understanding of this by asking them to pick out two or three key words which they think suggest the tone.

Activity 8 is intended to give your students some collaborative 'consider and reflect' time before using the additional material to inform further thinking in Activity 9. Make sure that you give students time to consider the issues raised by the prompts and to locate supporting evidence. At this stage, it is the evidence used to support their opinions which is important.

Activity 9 This activity also uses Text G.

Possible answers to 'what can you say about...'	
The man who has died and how he has died?	At home, whispering of fields unsown: suggests he was a farmer/from the countryside.
The tone of the first and second stanzas and the reasons for the differences in tone?	Until this morning and this snow: suggests he has frozen to death.

How the poet feels about the man's death?	The first stanza has a note of hope about it – that the warmth of the sun might just be enough to bring him back to life.
How the poet feels about war?	The second stanza is more angry and resentful of the pointlessness of Man's supposed rise to supremacy.
Why the poet chose the title 'Futility'?	• It is a wasteful/pointless/needless death. • War is wasteful of Man's ingenuity, of innocent lives. He feels we ought to be able to find better ways of using our intelligence. • 'Futility' summarises and reflects the sense of waste and pointlessness he feels.

Activities 10 and 11 This is an opportunity for students to pull together all their learning from the chapter to put together a developed response supported by evidence and extended commentary, because it is their opinion they must make sure that their opinion is supported by quotes from the text.

Activity 10 asks students for their opinion but their reasons should be based on their understanding of the poem, its context and the writer's viewpoint.

Check your learning Students should make a note to demonstrate their understanding of each of the terms given. Gather responses from around the class to clarify.

Plenary

Gather responses from around the class to clarify understanding of each point. Students should amend notes if necessary.

Outcomes

In this chapter your students have learned that:

• texts are often shaped by the time in history when they were written

• the culture or the kind of society in which the writer lives can affect what they write.

AO focus

English AO2 Reading and English language AO3 Studying written language

- Explain and evaluate how writers use linguistic, grammatical and structural features to achieve effects and engage and influence the reader.
- Develop and sustain interpretations of the writers ideas and perspectives.

In this chapter your students will:

- investigate the ways that writers create stories and how they get and keep their readers' attention, focusing on: openings, settings and endings
- evaluate the effectiveness of these tools.

Additional resources

Worksheets

6a: Openings

6b: Characters

6c: 'Crash'

6d: Setting

6e: Dialogue

6f: Contrast

6g: Endings

6h: A twist in the tale

Getting started

Start by asking students to think about the kinds of stories they have enjoyed. Explain that these do not have to be written stories. They could be films, spoken stories, fictional or non-fictional. Give a few examples of your own. Then allow students to talk for a couple of minutes in pairs and list their choices. Then ask them to talk about why they enjoyed them. Are they from a certain genre, for example, science fiction, or are they well told perhaps from the main character's perspective? Discuss what makes a good story.

Working through the chapter

Openings

(k) Viewpoints activity: Effective novel openings

Students will read two different openings – one using an action-packed event, the second introducing a main character. Explain that they are going to establish what makes them engaging and likely to sustain the interest of the reader.

Starting with action

As a class, read Text A: *Crash* (action) and get them to think about the impact of the first sentence. Contrast that with the second one. What are the features of each which help to make the impacts different?

Activity 1 This activity uses Text A: the opening to *Crash,* and Worksheet 6a.

This activity is about language choice and the impact on the audience.

a This part of the activity offers an opportunity to work with identified words and phrases. It should be a relatively short-burst activity – allow only 10–12 minutes for them to re-read and consider the five examples.

Things to look for:	
Story text	**Impact on audience**
'Then came the sickening thud on impact as the car folded like an empty coke can.'	'Thud' is onomatopoeic, which means it is very descriptive. It suggests a sudden impact. 'Sickening' suggests both an emotional **and** physical response to what has happened. If something is enough to make us feel sick then it must be bad. The use of the phrase 'the car folded like an empty coke can' provides a familiar reference image for the reader so that s/he can picture the ease with which the car crumpled under the impact.
'Jake was aware of all of this but powerless to respond.'	'Powerless' suggests that what was happening was beyond Jake's control. It is as though he is a helpless bystander looking on but unable to stop it happening.
'Every window shattered on impact and it rained glass.'	'Shattered' is much stronger than 'broke' or 'cracked'. It suggests that the windows completely disintegrated (almost exploded) because of the force of the crash. This is reinforced by the word 'rained', which gives the reader an impression of how many pieces of glass were in the air.
'For the first time, Jake felt pain as the steering wheel was thrust violently into his chest.'	'Thrust' and 'violently' suggest that Jake is on the receiving end of an act of some force/power/aggression.
'The pain was excruciating ...'	'Excruciating' is much stronger than 'hurt'. It suggests intense/agonising/unbearable pain – almost to the point of torture.

b Take class feedback and allow students to share their views on the quality of the opening. Remember that 'effectiveness' is, essentially, a matter of opinion so long as it is based on the text and supported by evidence.

Stretch yourself

A useful extension activity might ask students to look for other words/phrases and comment on them in the same ways and in the table.

Starting with characters

(k) Analysis activity: Introducing characters

Activity 2 This activity uses Text B: the opening to the story about Sam, and Worksheet 6b.

Possible answers	
a	**Things they should think about:**
	He moves: in a casual, easy way; he strides, which suggests confidence.
	He looks: tall; athletic; clean; stunning blue eyes (bright and alive with burning energy); he smiles and is polite (stands aside for her); he is held in high regard ('After all, this was Sam Clarke'); other girls like him ('tall, Clarke and handsome'.)
b	She likes and admires him – she blushes when he notices her.
c	Remember that 'effectiveness' is, essentially, a matter of opinion so long as it is based on the text and supported by evidence.

The bullet points encourage the students to consider the questions that have been posed by the introduction and how the writer uses words and phrases to engage the reader.

Activity 3 Worksheet 6c can be used with this activity. Students should use this to look back at Text A to think about the same sorts of issues. For example, students might consider:

- Will Jake survive?
- Where was he going?
- Will he be found?
- Who will find him?
- How old is he?

Setting

Planning activity: Interesting settings

The issue about Texts C and D is to develop the point about careful consideration of vocabulary.

Essentially, there is no right answer, it is about recognising the intended impact on the reader and how this is achieved.

Activities 4 and 5 These activities use Texts C and D, and Worksheet 6d.

Read the activities with students and encourage them to discuss what is being asked. It may be useful to model a response for the students by text marking one or two examples of the following:

- How the use of vocabulary differs.
- How the words carry impact, for example, the examples given in the table for the first sentence.
- A question that the text raises, for example, the ending of Text D does not indicate whether Jake is still alive).

You may wish to annotate the text using an interactive whiteboard or whiteboard. Then ask students to complete the exercise in pairs using the handout of the texts. Allow a few minutes and then take feedback and add to the class version on the board or on screen.

Some things to consider	
In Text C:	**In Text D:**
In the first sentence 'noise' and 'strangely' are rather vague.	In the first sentence 'sound and fury' and 'deathly quiet' create a stronger impression.
The second sentence offers more detail for clarity.	The second sentence is more vague – the simile is a bit 'tired'.
The third sentence is short for effect.	The third sentence is long – gives detail of the event – includes a simile for the tyre marks.
The fourth sentence breaks the 'rules' – begins with 'But' – but is deliberately short for effect.	The fourth sentence is much shorter – it breaks the rules – and returns to the 'quiet' of the first sentence.
The last sentence uses ellipses (…) to break the flow as it returns the reader's attention to Jake and his situation.	

Highlight that both texts use a mix of long and short sentences for effect. They also use some variation in sentence openings, for example, 'Trapped inside the car …' in Text C.

Dialogue

Activity 5 This activity uses Text E and Worksheet 6e.

Most of the revelations about the narrator appear in the final paragraph. They are in bold below.

'That afternoon, **I found it hard to concentrate** on Physics and Food Technology. **My head was spinning.** On the one hand, **I was a clumsy oaf,** who cannot even look where I am going. Then, when I have my big chance to talk to Sam, I manage three words, "Sorry", "Pardon" and "Alright". **He must think I am an idiot.** On the other hand, he did not react as most boys would and tell me to watch where I was going. And just what did he mean when he said, "I'll see you around" and "if you want to talk to me". Did *he* want to talk to *me*? Or was it just a figure of speech?'

Choose an example to model how to text mark and annotate the narrator's thoughts and feelings and their impact on the reader. Allow the pairs to work on completing the annotation and then to discuss Part c. Take feedback and discuss whether the text has sustained the interest of the students in the class. Allow the opportunity for students to update/amend their notes.

Things to look for:

- Sam: easy-going; sense of humour; ready smile.
- Narrator: could not concentrate; head spinning; worried about the impression she had created with him.
- Relationship: last three sentences suggest she is hopeful that he is interested in her and, therefore, that a relationship might develop.

Contrast

Activity 6 Worksheet 6f may be used for this activity. Activities 1–5 provide students with the tools needed to complete Activity 6, where they should look at:

- vocabulary choice
- sentence variety
- character development
- questions raised for the reader
- how *all* these help to develop the narrative.

Paragraph 1

a 'The motorway was like a war zone.' – this is a graphic and dramatic image, which suggests damage, debris and chaos.

b 'Policemen, firemen and paramedics …'

c Any of the following quotes would be appropriate:

- 'There were people and machines everywhere …'
- 'Three police cars blocked off the road and two policemen were in constant communication with base, keeping the road free of traffic and talking to the fire officers.'
- 'Two fire engines, parked on the hard shoulder.'
- 'They paced the tarmac anxiously, frequently glancing at the car and the paramedics …'
- 'Paramedics shuttled in and out to collect breathing apparatus, bandages and painkilling drugs.'
- 'The flashing lights from the vehicles cast eerie shadows on the road.'

Paragraph 2

a Different.

b 'Quietly' and 'motionless' help to create the contrast because they are the opposite of the words that were used in the first paragraph to create the effect of a busy, loud scene of an accident.

c The final sentence suggests that the situation will not end well. It creates a sense of suspense, the reader wants to read on to find out whether Jake survives or not.

Overall: paragraph 1 presents a more active, busy scene while paragraph 2 presents a scene which is serious and urgent but generally calmer and under control.

Each paragraph touches on the same question: will Jake survive? Paragraph 1 does this more through machines and technology while paragraph 2 achieves it through the efforts of the personnel working directly with Jake.

Endings

Move straight into the information on Student A's ending (Text G). Once again, you might want to remark on the way the story has been very carefully planned to create an impact on the reader. You could read the ending as a class. The last part of the Activity, (d), could be used as the basis of a class discussion on the ending.

Activity 7

Points for discussion	
a	What the dialogue reveals about Jake; the sense of urgency in what the medical team is saying; the build-up of tension as they fight to save his life – will they succeed?
b	The possibility of Jake being on his way to a birthday party; is Paula his girlfriend?; possibly makes the reader feel sad; raises the question of a senseless loss of a young life.
c	Encourage students to air their opinions and have a lively discussion about this. Make sure that they give reasons for their opinions.
d	As with effectiveness, this is a matter of opinion but should be supported by evidence from the text. It may be useful to open this up for a class discussion.

Activity 8

a Again, there is no right answer but they should be able to explain what it is *in the text* which guided their expectations.

b This is an opportunity for students to consider alternative endings for stories collaboratively. Reinforce the idea that only *one* of the possible developed endings should be based on their discussion for a).

Check your learning Here you might ask students to make a brief note about their understanding of each of the terms given and their effectiveness.

- Openings
- Setting
- Dialogue
- Endings

Plenary

Check learning and understanding by asking for feedback around the class. Allow the opportunity for students to update and amend their notes as necessary.

Outcomes

In this chapter your students have:

- investigated the ways that writers create stories
- investigated how writers get and keep their readers' attention, focusing on: openings, settings and endings
- evaluated the effectiveness of these tools.

7 Understanding arguments

AO focus

English AO2 Reading and English language AO3 Studying written language

- Develop and sustain interpretations of writers' ideas and perspectives.

- Explain and evaluate how writers use linguistic, grammatical, structural and presentational features to achieve effects and engage and influence the reader.

In this chapter your students will:

- learn how writers develop ideas using key points

- understand how writers use facts and statistics to support their opinion and persuade their audience

- examine the language writers use to influence their audience

- consider why expert opinions are used in an argument.

Additional resources

Worksheets

7a: Identifying key points

7b: Using emotive language

7c: Making a judgement about the writer's opinion

Getting started

The introduction demonstrates a process through which writers build an argument and communicate it to their readers. Ask the students to think about an activity they want to take part in that may require them to persuade their parents by arguing their case, for example, a stopover at a friend's house or a birthday party being held at a local club. Make them understand that they would not only have to consider the points they wanted to make but also *how* they were going to make them, in order to have maximum impact. Worksheet 7a can be used to support this activity. Give the class two minutes to think of points they could make to their parents then share them with the rest of the class.

Take their feedback and complete the column, 'key points'. Now encourage the students to work in pairs to complete the second column 'How

would they make the point?' It may be useful to make some suggestions, for example, 'I might say that all my friends would be there' or 'I might ask if they had any objections so that I could tackle them logically'. Allow two minutes or so for this activity. Now take feedback and complete the class table.

When the table is complete, make the point that the students have just gone through the process a writer would follow when writing an argument:

- thinking of key points

- thinking about how to make them.

Explain that the chapter will help them to read for meaning and then to analyse the writer's tactics.

Working through the chapter

Identifying key points

(k) Analysis activity: Arguments and language

The extract (Text A) on marketing food for children is used to show how writers present their views by introducing a key point and then reinforcing their opinion through exemplification and supportive details.

Though the key point may not always appear at the start of a paragraph it often does, making it easy to spot. The important thing is that students understand that a paragraph will have a key point somewhere and that the rest of the writing is designed to support it.

Activity 1 All activities use Text A.

This activity uses paragraphs 1–3 and Worksheet 7a.

This activity will help students to understand that arguments are organised into paragraphs and that each paragraph tends to have a main focus, followed by explanatory detail. When you start the tasks it may be helpful to read the first two paragraphs individually and ask the class to discuss the main point being made. You could then record their answers on the board. In short, this will mean that you are modelling how they should proceed with this task. Next, get the students to complete the tasks in pairs or individually. The table below provides possible answers for this activity.

Possible answers:	
a	It is made up of 'snack' foods; it lacks balance; he avoids healthy options like vegetables and salads.
b	• He is a target for bullying. • He is likely to have poor health in the future. • He is likely to have a shorter life expectancy. • He is likely to suffer from obesity, for example, with Type II diabetes. **Key point:** Jake's eating habits are putting his health at risk.
c	Obesity has doubled in the last ten years.
d	• The diet of young children is likely to cause health and social problems, such as bullying, in the future. • Their diets are not balanced. • Their diets are dominated by snack foods and very sugary or fatty foods.
e	• Paragraph 4: Companies are paying schools to allow them to target children with their high-sugar, high-fat foods in school. • Paragraph 5: Food companies target school canteens suggesting that if the foods are sold in school dining halls the staff must approve the products. • Paragraph 6: The writer is suggesting a link between the number of soft drinks children drink and hyperactivity. • Paragraph 7: If countries do not act quickly to encourage healthy eating, there will be a child health crisis caused by obesity.

Now you could take feedback and complete the class table. This may help to build class confidence.

Use of facts and statistics

(ki) Webquest activity: Reading and planning arguments

Activity 2 This activity uses paragraph 3.

Tell the class that they have been establishing the points the writer is making. Now they are going to look at the tactics s/he uses to make the points more convincing. Find out what the class already knows by asking what impact using facts and statistics is likely to have on a reader. They are likely to say that they add weight or credibility to the point being made.

Answers	
a	Obesity has doubled in the last ten years. / Health groups are warning of a crisis.
b	92% of children eat more saturated fat than the levels recommended.
c	It is likely to make them think about possible consequences for their own children and to consider their children's diet.
d	Whole class sharing enables students to modify/clarify their thinking. It also provides an opportunity to ascertain their readiness to move on.

Before moving on you might want to establish with the class that all of the facts in the article are 'negative' in that they are painting a very worrying picture of the health of young people. Ask them if they think that is a fair or complete picture of the situation. They may say that it is a biased or unbalanced view. Make the point that they have been carefully selected to support the writer's case. Suggest that a writer could make a very different point about children's health simply by choosing a different set of facts and statistics; for example, the influence of food technology lessons and the plethora of television cookery shows mean that young people have never been more aware of what is good for them.

Using emotive language

Students need to understand that it is not words themselves that are emotive but the way the writer uses them. You could demonstrate this through exploring their reactions to the use of the words 'small grey' in the following sentences: 'The small grey child slumped listlessly in the corner.' 'The small grey handbag stood temptingly in the shop window.'

Activity 3 This activity uses paragraphs 4–5 and Worksheet 7b.

a It is likely that students will focus on 'worried' and 'angry'. They may want to use their own words such as 'let down' or even 'cheated'. The main point to reinforce here is the need to use the text to justify their opinion. Allow the students to select words they want to use for this activity and then model how to write a sentence or two using textual reference to support the point. *Justification* is the important thing and the activity could provide opportunity for them to discuss this in paired/small group/whole class situations.

b The activity is designed to lead students to engage with the fine details of text to determine the writer's viewpoint.

The modelled part of the response table shows how they might start to interpret the language used.

Their own responses might touch on:

• 'as young as four': the fact that it shows children as young as four being used to test these sugary products highlights their vulnerability – they are like guinea pigs.

• 'The marketing kit boasts': this is happening away from parents; to suggest that school staff approve of what is happening and implying it is underhand. Yet the company is 'boasting' of this practice, suggesting little concern for the health of the children.

Using expert opinion

Activity 4 This activity uses paragraph 7.

Tell students that they are being asked to *interpret* the impact of the expert's views. Remind them that they are being asked to think about the way parents will react to these opinions. Begin by reading the paragraph aloud. Ask a student to suggest on opinion that is being expressed. Now ask the class to suggest the possible impact of that view on a parent. Worksheet 7b can be used to record their ideas, an example of the table is provided below in case the worksheet is unavailable.

Views of Philip James	Possible impact on parents
Overall impact of using these views as a final paragraph.	

Answers	
a	• There are up to five distinct points to make here though students may well have grouped two or more together. • Europe is going to suffer a huge increase in childhood obesity. • Britain is the country with the most serious childhood obesity problem. • The incidence of childhood diabetes will grow alarmingly (hospital wards will be full). • Major health problems among people in their thirties will increase greatly. • Countries in Europe must act quickly to prevent a crisis.
b	• Students might say that parents may be shocked, worried, or stirred into taking more care over their children's diets. Remind them to justify their answers by referring to the text.
c	• In the article, the author aims to raise awareness and warn parents about the problem of childhood obesity. The last paragraph comprises an alarming set of opinions. This strongly reinforces his view and is the last thing the reader reads.

Making a judgement about the writer's opinion

Viewpoints activity: Effective arguments

Activity 5 This activity uses Worksheet 7c.

This is an opportunity to give some additional purpose to what has gone before, allowing students to consider and present their own views on the topic they have been studying. It could also provide an opportunity for rehearsal for a Speaking and listening assessment.

At the end of the group task you might want to give the class a 'big question' to think about

and then to discuss. For example: 'Should we be worried by the article in *The Observer*?'

Allow students to make a list of points they might want to express. A minute or two for this is sufficient. They should work on their own for this part of the process. It is *their* opinion that is being sought. If at all possible, the class should form a circle so that they can see each other. Explain that they are going to discuss the 'big question'.

The following rules should be explained:

- One person will start the process by expressing her/his point of view. That person will have a 'symbol of authority' as speaker, for example, a pen, a ball, a trophy.

- A speaker should end by asking a general question and asking someone to volunteer to answer it *or* by nominating another speaker and by passing on the symbol of authority.

- Explain that if a person wants to contribute s/he should indicate that to the current speaker.

- No-one should make a contribution of more than 45 seconds.

- The teacher will not express a view but may choose to intervene to nominate a speaker or to ask a question.

- The teacher will keep a record of points made for a plenary at the end.

This kind of discussion will build confidence and engagement and foster independent thinking. It will also allow students to draw on evidence they have selected from the reading, to evaluate its merit and to justify their views if challenged. It is crucial that the thinking time at the beginning of the process is observed. In this way, every student should have something to contribute if nominated.

Check your learning

Preparation

The tasks in this section are both 'how' questions. Explain that the first task does not simply ask for examples of fact, statistics and opinion but for an explanation of how they are used. In the same way, the second task requires an explanation of how the writer deliberately selects language to have an impact on the reader. Remind students to think about the writer's purpose: to inform, persuade and influence the reader. They could text mark facts, statistics and opinions using different colours and then work out the balance of fact and opinion and discuss, in pairs, how they are used, in combination, to influence the reader. For the second task, they could use a further colour to highlight words and phrases that are used to affect the way the reader thinks. Once again, a paired discussion of the likely impact of the chosen phrases will help to clarify the students' thoughts.

Responses

In both tasks, students are required to:

- Make a point, for example, 'the writer uses expert opinion to influence the reader's opinion about the dangers of children's diet …'

- Use evidence/quotation to support the point being made.

- Explain/analyse the intended impact on the reader of the words chosen as evidence.

When the students have completed these tasks, and before assessing their progress, ask the students, in pairs, to use the margin to highlight 'point', 'evidence' and 'analysis'. You could pre-empt this by asking one or two students to present their answers on an interactive whiteboard and model this approach, focusing on the quality of the analysis, pointing out good practice and suggesting improvements. The class should then identify 'golden lines' from their partners' work and be prepared to read them out, explaining why they are examples of good analysis.

Plenary

Give the students the following headings: Key Points, Facts and Statistics, Expert Opinion and Language.

The students, in pairs are to write four sentences in which they explain how each of these features is used by an author to create a convincing argument. Pairs should exchange sentences and discuss any differences. The teacher should then take feedback and consolidate the learning.

Outcomes

In this chapter your students have:

- understood how writers deliberately construct an argument

- understood the terms: 'key points', 'facts' and 'statistics', 'expert opinion', 'language'.

- actively read and analysed texts

- participated in a group discussion about *The Observer* article

- participated in reflective paired discussion

- peer assessed written tasks.

8 Responding to texts

AO focus

**English AO2 Reading and English Language
AO3 Studying written language**

Develop and sustain interpretation of writers' ideas and perspectives.

In this chapter your students will:

- understand how and why writers use facts and opinions

- examine how writers use words to influence the reader

- explore how a writer's point of view is revealed by the words they choose.

Additional resources

Worksheets

8a: Fact and opinion

8b: Writer's point of view

8c: 'The "Bore" Lords'

8d: Using words to influence the reader

8e: Recognising the writer's viewpoint

Getting started

Before you start work on this chapter it may be useful to initiate some class discussion about the difference between fact and opinion. You may wish to have an example of each written on the board and use those to start the discussion or you could ask students to suggest five facts and five opinions of their own for each of the following:

- myself

- my best friend

- my favourite hobby

- my favourite TV programme/music/film/pop star/actor/school subject/teacher

- my favourite animal.

Collect contributions from around the class and gauge understanding of the difference. Be sure to have clear definitions and examples for students who may be confused by the differences. The facts and opinions do not have to be serious, so you can let the students be as creative as they like.

Working through the chapter

Fact and opinion

🔲 Learning activity: Fact and opinion

This introduction is designed largely to establish the difference between facts and opinions.

Activity 1 This activity considers the difference between fact and opinion, and uses Worksheet 8a.

Fact and opinion answers	
Fact	**Opinion**
Julius Caesar was a Roman Emperor.	*Big Brother* is the worst programme on TV.
Hadrian's Wall passed through Northumberland and Cumbria.	Visiting an art museum is a good way to spend an afternoon.
Skiing is one of the most popular sports in Switzerland.	Eating meat is wrong.

Activity 2 This activity uses Text B: 'Facts about Rome' and Worksheet 8b.

Students should be encouraged to consider the following issues:

- A writer will select facts which reflect his/her point of view.

- Some facts can be used to support both negative and positive viewpoints, for example, the temperature and late opening restaurants. These can be interpreted in two ways, positive – if you want to relax in the cool of the evening after a hot day's sightseeing – or negative – if the noise keeps you from getting to sleep after a tiring day!

You could ask students to try out this dual purpose idea with some other facts about Rome and/or some of their own facts from the starter activity. Ensure that your students have a clear understanding of how facts are selected to reflect opinion by asking them to explain their choices.

Activity 3 This activity uses Text C and Worksheet 8c.

Paragraph 1 is modelled for students; clarify their grasp of facts and opinions and how they are used (part b) before allowing them to move on to paragraph 2.

Answers on 'The "Bore" Lords' paragraphs 1 and 2 (Text C)

a   Opinion in paragraph 1
- long awaited
- massive disappointment
- handsome
- ruthless
- unrealistic
- which made even the 1970s *Star Trek* look action-packed.

Facts in paragraph 1
- fantasy tale, set in the mythical land of Arkon
- played by Ben Knight
- plot sees Knight thrown into a dungeon and falsely accused of being a traitor by the king
- Knight becomes a fugitive, trying to clear his name and save the kingdom before it is too late.

b   What each opinion says about the writer's point of view in paragraph 1.
- long awaited: suggests that it *could* be genuine
- massive disappointment: suggests that it did not live up to expectations and was not worth the wait
- handsome: suggests the hero
- ruthless: suggests the 'baddy'
- unrealistic: suggests that it was beyond belief – not convincing
- made even the 1970s *Star Trek* look action packed: suggests that it was old-fashioned and amateurish.

c   Opinion in paragraph 2
- at least fifty minutes too long
- lengthy, dull
- more like a worrier than a warrior
- should stick to delivering funny lines rather than saving the universe.

d   This is an opportunity to consolidate understanding through their explanation.

Using words to influence the reader

Viewpoints activity: The writer's influence

This section of the chapter is intended to show how word choice impacts on the impression created for the reader. It connects with how writers use (or do not use) facts and how the same facts may have a dual purpose, it is the adverbs and adjectives which reflect viewpoint

and purpose when presenting facts and opinions. You might ask students to try replacing the words in bold in the two sentences to retain the same sense of differing impressions in the two headlines.

Activity 4 This activity uses Worksheet 8d. There are no right or wrong answers here so long as each headline pairing gives a differing impression from the other one. This activity provides another opportunity for students to share their ideas and clarify their understanding.

Stretch yourself
As an additional activity, you may ask pairs of students to write five headlines of their own and then swap them with their partner to see if they can change them to give yet another impression.

Recognising the writer's viewpoint

Analysis activity: Identifying the writer's viewpoint

Use the first paragraph of Text E to model how words and phrases might be interpreted so as to gain an understanding of the writer's viewpoint.

Activity 5 This activity uses Text E and Worksheet 8e.

It enables students to apply their understanding from the modelled first paragraph annotations to paragraphs 2 and 3. Ask students to use the model to look at the highlights in the following paragraphs and make similar comments for each of them. You could have different pairs of students working on different paragraphs.

Points for consideration - Trafford Centre analysis (Text E)	
PHRASE	**COMMENT / IMPLICATIONS**
'like bees to a honey pot'	This suggests that the Centre is irresistible – it is almost as though they cannot help themselves.
'to trudge up and down the malls'	The word 'trudge' suggests it is hard work – no real enjoyment in it.
'a crowd scene that looks like the neighbouring Old Trafford Football Ground on a match day.'	It is *very* busy – people are everywhere – quite chaotic.
'they marvel at'	The shoppers appear to be overawed / overcome by the splendour of what they see.

Phrase	Comment/implications
'So much like the same store in their own town'	Together with the statement above* it is the tone which is important here – the writer is poking fun at the idea of people going all the way to the Trafford Centre only to end up with the same shops they have in their home town.
'you can always rely on Macdonald's'	People stay with the 'tried and tested' rather than be adventurous and try something new or different.
'they display their shopping'	The shopping is like a prize to be shown off with pride so that others may see.
'their reward for braving the crowds'	Makes it sound as though it is something to be endured – not pleasurable.
'to count the cost of their wonderful day out.'	The key word here is 'wonderful' and it is ironic – the writer does not think the day out is wonderful at all – but it is expensive.
'shopping heaven!'	The exclamation mark suggests this is ironic – it is nothing like heaven really.

Stretch yourself

An extension activity could ask students to annotate the rest of Text E as they have seen for paragraph 1.

Writing about viewpoint

The information in this section provides the 'Point – Proof – Comment' model for students to use when they are writing about a writer's viewpoint. The point about Activity 6 is to show students how to develop their thinking and express it in an extended, coherent way.

Activity 6 This activity enables students to apply the model demonstrated in the developed student response (Text F). The annotation provides a framework of 'criteria' against which

students are able to judge their own responses for Activity 7.

Activity 7 Text G: the student evaluation, supports this activity.

a   Students undertake a short-burst writing activity to demonstrate their understanding of the developed response. Students should use the framework provided as part of Text F and Text G to help them to shape the response.

b   This is an opportunity for some peer assessment. Students should use the framework as the measure of how successful their partner has been in constructing the response.

Allow opportunity for students to amend/improve their responses following feedback from their partner.

Plenary

Check your learning   As with any plenary session, this is about clarifying what students have understood in the chapter and gauging whether they have grasped the learning objectives.

a   This is a review of what they have learned. You could take some group/class responses to check for understanding and clarity.

b   This section aims to consolidate skills through application to another text. Students should use the framework to help them to shape the response. Students could peer assess the responses as in 7b above using the framework as the measure of how successful their partner has been in constructing the response.

Outcomes

In this chapter your students have learnt to:

● understand how and why writers use facts and opinions

● examine how writers use words to influence the reader

● explore how a writer's point of view is revealed by the words s/he chooses.

AO focus

English AO2 Reading and English Language
AO3 Studying written language

Develop and sustain interpretation of writers' ideas and perspectives.

In this chapter your students will:

- develop their ideas about texts
- explore the author's viewpoint
- learn how to explain their ideas using evidence.

Additional resources

Worksheets

9a: Following clues to the writer's viewpoint 1

9b: Following clues to the writer's viewpoint 2

9c: Understanding the writer's viewpoint – Sorrento

9d: Understanding the writer's viewpoint – Sousse

Getting started

It may be appropriate to start with the illustration. You could ask students to predict where they think the boy might be going, what they can glean from his body language, and what the setting adds to their understanding of the situation. They could work in pairs to discuss these questions and then share their ideas with the class.

Working through the chapter

Following clues

(k!) Viewpoints activity: Finding the writer's viewpoint in newspapers

Activity 1 This activity uses Text A and Worksheet 9a.

After reading Text A the students are now in a position to see if their predictions are borne out. Once again, pair work might be productive here. Encourage pairs to discuss the following:

- The boy's concerns about the relationship with his girlfriend now she is moving to London.
- His worries about the scene that might ensue with his parents.

Students might pick out words like 'trudged', 'hell to pay' and 'slow plod' as being indicative of his tiredness, depression and sense of foreboding. You may wish to provide the opportunity for whole class discussion at this point.

Activity 2 This activity uses Text B and Worksheet 9b.

After the students have read Text B, allow them a couple of minutes to think about their answer to the question in Activity 2. This 'thinking' time should enable the students to provide more developed suggestions, which may include the following:

- The darkness, the noise of the snapping twig, the boy's unease 'not my preferred route', 'I told myself I had imagined the sound', 'shivering slightly'.
- The writer might want the reader to feel uneasy and tense, worried for the boy, sympathetic, etc.

It may be helpful to take some feedback from the class before moving on to the worked example. You may want to make the point that the quote is the starting point for the writer's interpretation of what the boy may be thinking. This is a model for their responses.

Activity 3 Now move on to the three quotes within the activity. There are two things to highlight to students here. Worksheet 9b may also be used here.

First, they are being asked to interpret a text and phrases like the following show that they are expressing a point of view about what is going on in the story.

'This suggests …'; 'This makes me think …'; 'This gives the reader the idea that …'

Point out these phrases as useful in this kind of writing.

Secondly, the task asks for more than one possible interpretation for each quote.

You may decide to work through the first quote as a class and raise the following points:

'Soon she would be off to London and he would be left.' The suggestion is that he is bothered by his girlfriend's impending move to London. Could it be that he is worried about the impact on the relationship or might it be that he is worried that she is moving on in life and he is standing still, or both?

You could model an answer to this task on the board, using the stem suggested in the task. This will mean the students have a written example in the book and one that you have modelled with them. Now they can work individually on the rest of the activity. It may be useful to allow five or six minutes for this task and then ask students to work in pairs to check over each other's work. You could ask for some volunteers to read out/ present their responses and encourage the class to find strengths and areas for improvement in the answers. A starting point may be 'Does the answer explore what might be suggested by the quote?'

Clues and culture

Analysis activity: Texts from other cultures

Read the opening text explaining cultural background and its possible impact on a text. Make sure that the class is comfortable with the term 'cultural background'. Suggest things that might be used to help identify the culture of a place such as accent, dialect, housing, typical jobs, foods, sports and pastimes etc. Ask the students to consider their own region and what makes up its culture, for example, inner city, lots of flats, ethnic mix, religious diversity, some unemployment, strong 'Brummie' accent etc. Links could also be forged here with Unit 3: the Spoken language section.

Activity 4 Encourage the students to read the biographical information on Tatamkhulu Afrika. The point of this reading is to develop an understanding of how Afrika's own experiences have influenced his writing. The TRUE/FALSE task is a way of establishing that the students have successfully understood the events of his life.

The answers are:

i True iv False

ii False v True

iii True

Activity 5 The poem 'Nothing's Changed' (Text C) could be read and the first question discussed as a whole class activity, then the students could discuss the other questions. This may be best tackled in pairs, with each pair then teaming up with another pair to compare what they have identified. This process will build confidence and independence.

Points to look for		
	Question	Possible answer
a	The first stanza helps the reader to picture the scene. What kind of scene is it?	Derelict, overgrown, poorly maintained
b	Think about the phrase 'amiable weeds'. How does the writer seem to think about this place?	They add detail to support the idea of a neglected area: litter strewn, overgrown with weeds, loose stones, etc. The word 'amiable' may suggest a certain affection for the place because of its part in his upbringing.
c	How does the writer show that this place is important to who he is?	It is a part of his upbringing and even his 'feet' recognise he is in District Six. He does not need to be told by any sign.
d	How does he get a sense of his anger across to the reader?	He is angry at the way the place has been allowed to decay: He uses words like, 'the soft labouring of my lungs' to imply that he is beginning to breathe heavily as he becomes angered. Also 'the hot, white inward turning anger of my eyes' reflects the heat of his rage when he considers his inner feelings about the place and its condition.
e	What do the words 'Brash with glass', 'flaring like a flag' and 'squats' tell us about the poet's feelings about the new restaurant?	These words all suggest that the restaurant is ostentatious (brash, flaring like a flag), and taking over an area where it should not be (squats). The word 'flaring' might suggest how its very presence makes him angry.
f	What does the poet mean by the words: 'we know where we belong'? How has the poet drawn particular attention to this stanza?	He is stating that this is not a restaurant for non-whites. This is a sign that although apartheid has ended, the racial divide still exists. By separating this pair of lines from the rest of the poem, he is drawing attention to its significance in the way he is thinking.

Points to look for		
	Question	**Possible answer**
g	What kind of restaurant is described here?	It is a place for fine dining, expensive décor and furnishings: beautiful linen, crystal glass, flowers.
h	In what ways is this eating place different to that described in stanza 5?	It serves cheap, basic food (Bunny Chows) and it has very basic plastic furniture.
i	What does the poet suggest about the people who eat here?	This is a café for the poor blacks. They can only afford to eat very basic, greasy food. Eating for these people is about sustenance and not fine dining.
j	What different things does the poet feel when he looks through the glass of the posh restaurant?	It reawakens all his old feelings of anger and makes him feel rebellious. It causes him to realise that though apartheid has gone, little has changed in society. The poor blacks have little more than before. He is frustrated and his urge to destroy is strong.

Take whole class feedback on the answers.

Activity 6: In this activity students will need to use evidence from the text to interpret what the writer felt. This is an important part of the chapter because this task reflects the kind of writing students will be expected to produce in an exam or controlled assessment. Point out the importance of the bullet points in the activity because the bullets provide the direction they will need to follow if they are to produce a well-rounded answer.

Understanding the writer's perspective

Text D and Text F reflect very different attitudes to the places visited. Students are going to use these texts to complete a table of key criteria for helping to judge the author's viewpoint. These key criteria are:

- opening comments
- descriptive details
- closing comments (Text F).

These will be used to support an answer about how the writer conveys his viewpoint to the

reader. You could start by explaining and clarifying these criteria so that students understand what they are going to do when they are faced with the texts and the table. Then you could move on to a class reading of Text D.

Activity 7 This activity uses Text D and Worksheet 9c.

a It may be useful to ask for initial thoughts about the writer's attitude to the place. Prompt students to consider what specifically the writer likes about the places. Introduce Worksheet 9c and ask students to text mark words and phrases that convey the writer's thoughts. Show them how to identify, text mark and annotate the writer's use of devices and vocabulary; for example, Sorrento is the jewel in Italy's crown (metaphor) suggests distinct, precious, a thing of beauty. Ensure that the students have time to work in pairs on the text and after completion encourage pairs to share their views with the rest of the class.

b Now it may be helpful to introduce the table and direct students to work through the 'Opening lines' section, which has already been completed, to explain how to complete the table. As a class, complete some of the 'Descriptive details' box and then, in pairs, get the students to complete the rest of the table and take feedback.

Writing your own interpretation

🄺 Planning activity: Viewpoints in travel writing

Activity 8 This activity uses Text F and Worksheet 9d. The key thing in this section is to point out that students should explain what is being said in the text and explore its possible impact on the reader. Run through the modelled text and its annotations. Be clear about the importance of words and phrases such as 'makes it sound', 'as though he wants the reader to' and 'maybe'.

Allow students five to ten minutes to complete the text marking and table completion task on the Sousse text and highlight the importance of the bullets.

Check your learning When completed, allow students ten minutes to write their answer to the question. Finally, get the students to, in pairs, text mark their own work. They should use the bullet points to guide their marking. They could use different colours to show where they have addressed each bullet point. You may wish to model this process before the students start this task. Ensure sufficient time is allowed to read some of the responses and discuss how they have:

- addressed the bullet points
- expressed their views clearly

- used evidence
- reflected on how the quotes selected convey the author's views.

Stretch yourself

More able students may enjoy the challenge of practising the process of text marking and writing/discussing other texts. The more they practise the better they will become. You should use a range of short texts to include poems, extracts from stories, newspaper or magazine articles, and biographies.

Plenary

Divide the class into groups of four. Provide each group with a sheet of paper. Ask them to complete a list of top tips for students learning to understand and write about a writer's views in a text. Ask them to focus on:

- things to look for in a text
- rules to follow when explaining a writer's views.

You might give a couple of examples to get them started; for example, text mark opinions, use words like 'suggests' in your answers. Allow five minutes to complete and then ask for feedback. Create a class set of tips and display it in class for future reference.

Outcomes

- Understanding of how to scan text for opinion, use of vocabulary, factual detail, etc.
- Knowledge of how to text mark and annotate text.
- Active involvement in reading and annotation of texts.
- Understanding of key conventions of writing about author's viewpoint.
- Reflective paired discussion about authorial viewpoint.
- Peer assessment of written tasks.
- Extension – self-directed study of further texts.

10 Comparing texts

AO focus

English AO2 Reading and English Language AO3 Studying written language

Read and understand texts, selecting material appropriate to purpose, collating from different sources and making comparisons and cross-references as appropriate.

In this chapter your students will:

- learn how to make comparisons between texts
- find similarities and differences between texts
- plan and write a comparison.

Additional resources

Worksheets

10a: Making a comparison

10b: Mobile phone advertisements

10c: The language of comparison

10d: 'The Thickness of Ice'

10e: Comparing poems 1

10f: Comparing poems 2

Getting started

This section is designed to ensure that students understand that comparisons are based on objective criteria. This applies to poetry but also to real life comparisons. You might ask them to talk about the way comparison websites are set out. Explain that when we look at the prices quoted, we have to be sure that they are covering all we want them to; that is, that they are using the same criteria as those we require. Now ask the class to list five things they would only buy after they had compared the products on offer, for example, ipod, television.

Take feedback and when you have a reasonable list, ask the students, in pairs, to think about one item and to decide what they would be looking for in that product. Ask pairs to read out their ideas and provide comments. Establish that the things they would use to judge a product are called 'criteria' and that comparison involves using the criteria to make judgements about each product and their relative similarities and differences. This should lead naturally into the opening section of the Student Book.

Working through the chapter

Making a comparison

🔟 Analysis activity: Comparing non-fiction texts 1

🔟 Learning activity: Comparing non-fiction texts 2

The key to this part of the lesson is to enable students to explore the idea that, in making judgements about something or between two things, we do it on the basis of considering important features or *criteria*. Worksheet 10a can be used as a starter activity.

Activity 1 This activity asks students to begin to identify key features which might inform their judgement about something, in this case, mobile phones.

Activities 2 and 3 These activities use Text A and Text B, two mobile phone advertisements.

This is an opportunity for students to rehearse the skills of establishing, identifying and comparing appropriate features/criteria and use them to inform their response to Activity 3. The table is a means by which they are able to bring their thoughts together in a form which is more easily managed. In combination, these activities walk the students through a process that they will apply in Activity 4. The table, the texts and the activity are available in Worksheet 10b.

The language of comparison

Text C is a modelled response showing how this sort of writing is constructed using a mixture of textual detail and personal opinion together with the 'language of comparison'.

Worksheet 10c could be given to the students as an exemplar from which to work in constructing their own writing. This is to raise awareness/reinforce knowledge of the types of words that should populate writing of this sort.

Activity 4 This activity uses Text C

This brings Activities 1, 2 and 3 together by giving students a purpose and audience for their writing.

Peer assessment allows students to apply the criteria they identified in informing their judgements and the use of the vocabulary appropriate to the language of comparison.

Comparing poems

(k) Planning activity: Comparing poems

Having established the principle of using criteria through working with non-literary material, students are now moving on to apply their understanding to literary material. Here, broad criteria have been provided for them.

A pdf of the poem 'The Thickness of Ice' by Liz Loxley (Text D), is available online for students in Worksheet 10d.

Activity 5 This activity uses Text D.

Answers

a The three stages are:
   - Stage 1 – stanzas 1 and 2: meeting as friends and testing the relationship to see if there is some strength in it.
   - Stage 2 – stanzas 3 and 4: as they become more comfortable with each other they do not try as hard to impress or please the other person; as the relationship begins to crumble each will look out for him/herself rather than be concerned for the other.
   - Stage 3 – stanzas 5 and 6: after the relationship fails and they are no longer friends, there will be resentment and jealousy; they will be cautious.

b Relationships in general; the first line says, 'We'll (we will) meet as friends', suggesting a meeting with someone has yet to take place at some point in the future; the rest of the poem continues to use the future tense and talking about events as though it is inevitable that they *will* happen.

c - Bitter about a failed relationship – it is *possible* that this is what has shaped the views of the writer.
   - Resigned to the fact that most relationships fail in the end – as the writer appears to be talking about relationships in general, this could be the impression she has of how most relationships tend to evolve.
   - Convinced that love will last for ever – no.
   - When things go wrong, we think about ourselves first, in stanza 4 she says: '(And one day when the ice gives way <u>we will scramble to save ourselves and not each other)</u>'.
   - None of these – students would need to have *very* convincing reasons to choose this option.

d - 'testing the thickness of ice' – as skaters want to be sure the ice is strong enough to support them and keep them safe from harm, so people entering into a relationship want the same sense of security from the other person.
   - 'less eager than the skater going for gold' – the skater who wants to win will try as hard as they can to succeed but, as a relationship develops, people are less prepared to put real effort into keeping it strong than they were at the start when they really wanted the relationship to work.
   - 'the creeping cracks will be ignored' – cracks in the ice are a warning to the skater that things are going wrong and there is danger if the warning is ignored; similarly, in a relationship, if warning signs that things are not right are ignored, there is a danger that it will fail.

e It is the justification which is important here. This could be used as a sharing activity, allowing students to explore, explain and clarify their thinking.

f Students should identify features such as:
   - chronological sequence tracking the development of relationships
   - the use of brackets to reveal the thoughts of the writer
   - the way the poem is written is (almost) conversational
   - the rhythm is consistent though stanza form varies.

g Again, it is the justification which is important. This could also be used as a sharing activity, allowing students to explore, explain and clarify their thinking.

h This response is a personal opinion, so there is no right answer – it is the justification which is important and the evidence used in support.

Activity 6 The table and this activity are available in Worksheet 10e.

As with the similar table used to compare the mobile phones in Activity 2, this table allows students to make their findings more manageable, making it easier to make comparisons and informed judgements.

Activity 7 A pdf of the poem 'I never said I loved you, John' by Christina Rosetti (Text E) is available online for students in Worksheet 10f.

Answers

a Students might comment on some of the following details:
   - 'Why will you tease me day by day'
   This suggests he keeps pestering her about showing her love for him.
   - 'do' and 'pray'?
   This suggests he wants her to think about their relationship.
   - 'a face as wan
   As shows an hour-old ghost?'
   This suggests his feelings are making him look pale and sickly.
   - 'don't remain single for my sake'

This implies he has suggested that she is the *only* woman for him.

● 'I have no heart?'

This suggests he has accused her of being cruel/ unfeeling.

● 'Don't call me false'

This accuses her of misleading him about her feelings for him.

● 'I'll wink at your untruth'

This suggests he has falsely accused her of saying that she loves him.

b Here are five answers that students may select.

● I never said I loved you, John:
● And wax a weariness to think upon
  No fault of mine made me your toast:
● I dare say Meg or Moll would take
  Pity upon you, if you'd ask:
● But then you're mad to take offence
  That I don't give you what I have not got:
● I'd rather answer 'No' to fifty Johns
  Than answer 'Yes' to you.
● Catch at today, forget the days before:

c This is about personal opinion but justification should be based on textual detail.

d The intended effect is that the reader sees the situation from the woman's point of view and therefore sympathises with her as she is being pursued by the man and she does not want his attentions.

e The order of events: not as relevant here as in the previous poem.

Stanzas: the poem has a regular stanza pattern.

Rhythm and rhyme: the poem has a regular ABAB rhyme scheme and a regular rhythm with each stanza having 8-8-10-6 syllables per line.

f It is the justification which is important here. This part could be used as a sharing activity, allowing students to explore, explain and clarify their thinking.

g This response is a personal opinion so there is no right answer. What is important is that the students justify and use evidence to support their answers.

Activity 8 This activity allows students to build an 'evidence base' which they are going to use to compare the two poems and help them to make some judgements about them. Working with a partner and sharing their responses helps the students to consolidate knowledge and clarify their understanding. Asking the students to find the similarities and differences leads them to the brink of a written response.

Writing the response

This section of the chapter gives students structure to help them build a response.

Activity 9 This provides the students with the opportunity to apply their learning in a short-burst writing activity. The peer assessment aspect helps students to use the criteria for this sort of writing to make a judgement about how well they have succeeded.

The mnemonic ELM can be a helpful aide-memoire to reinforce learning.

Stretch yourself

This activity is intended to extend and sharpen the way that students think about comparison of poems. Encourage students to discuss their views of the poems. A useful prompt question could be: Which is the most effective poem?

Check your learning This produces an opportunity to review the learning from the chapter.

Plenary

Direct students to work in pairs to list criteria that could be used to compare one of the following:

● Cars for a family with three children under eleven.
● A holiday for the same family.
● Television, broadband and telephone packages for the home.

At least two groups should share the same subject. Students should have one minute to complete the task. The teacher should take feedback and reinforce the idea that the students have produced objective criteria for a comparison and that effective comparison relies on this approach.

Outcomes

In this chapter your students have:

● understood how comparisons are based on objective criteria
● understood the language of comparison and its place in comparative study
● been actively involved in reading and analysis of texts
● written comparisons of both literary and non-literary texts
● participated in reflective paired discussion about texts
● peer-assessed written tasks.

11 Making your reading skills count in the exam

AO focus

English AO2 Reading and English Language AO3 Studying written language

- Read and understand texts, selecting material appropriate to purpose, collating from different sources and making comparisons and cross-references as appropriate.
- Develop and sustain interpretations of writers' ideas and perspectives.
- Explain and evaluate how writers use linguistic, grammatical, structural and presentational features to achieve effects and engage and influence the reader.

English AO2 only

- Understand texts in their social, cultural and historical contexts.

In this chapter your students will:

- learn more about how their reading will be tested in the exam
- study sample questions and answers
- look at how responses can be improved.

Additional resources

Worksheets

11a: Sample questions

11b: Sample answers

11c: Your response

Getting started

In this section of the book students will learn about the reading part of the examination they will take as part of their GCSE English or English Language course. They will have the opportunity to look at the kinds of questions they will be asked to answer and see how their work will be marked. The advice and comments of an experienced examiner will guide them through what follows.

It is always difficult to convey to students the important information, such as the facts and details, included in this section, but it is vital to their success.

To begin with, there are several key facts to emphasise about the length of the examination, the number of items they will be expected to read, the number of questions etc. Many students are inclined to gloss over this type of information, when it is important that they engage with it.

It may be helpful to consider some of the following suggestions for ways of engaging your students with this important information.

You could ask the students to read the information in the section 'About the exam'. Tell them it contains 13 key facts about the reading section of the paper. Ask them to work in pairs to produce a list of the key facts. To make it more challenging you could set them a time limit. Then take a fact from each pairing until you run out. The element of competition or challenge will engage and focus the thoughts of most students.

The answers	
1	There is one exam paper in GCSE English and GCSE English Language.
2	Its focus is: Understanding and producing non-fiction texts.
3	The paper is divided into two sections.
4	The reading section should take one hour.
5	The reading section is worth 20% of your final marks.
6	The reading section contains four non-fiction items.
7	Students will be asked to answer six questions.
8	There will be at least one question on each item.
9	The final question will ask candidates to compare two items of their choice.
10	The comparison question will ask candidates to focus on a particular feature such as presentational features or use of language.
11	The non-fiction items are likely to be taken from magazines, newspapers, books, leaflets, advertisements and/or web pages.
12	Candidates will be able to make notes or highlight key points on the items provided.
13	An answer booklet will be provided, containing the questions and a space for answers.

Assessment Objectives

The following section of the chapter sets out the Assessment Objectives with explanations of the key words such as 'understand, collate, cross references, evaluate' etc. It is important that students understand the skills on which they are going to be assessed. There are some quite difficult ideas to grasp in this section. If students seem to be confused or unsure of what all of these terms mean, you may want to suggest that the exam will examine their ability to:

● follow the writer's argument, select points being made and explain them

● select ideas from more that one item and bring them together in one answer

● read between the lines and work out what a writer thinks or may be suggesting about a subject

● explain the way a text is presented or how the writer uses language and say how effective they think it is

● explain how the writer is trying to influence the way the reader thinks about a subject.

Working through the chapter

Sample questions

You may want to introduce the key to the skills being tested, featured after the questions, before examining the specimen questions as this should help to make sense of the letters next to each one. An opportunity to use sample examination papers, as they are made available by the examination board, would allow the class to read the questions and apply the letters from the key in order, to consolidate their understanding of question types.

Tips for students:

Each question has a command word that specifies the kind of response that is needed. Share these with the student:

Questions 1, 2

Words and phrases like: 'Give four ...' or 'List' require a point per mark on offer. Students are being tested on their ability to find and retrieve information.

Question 3

'Choose' indicates how many examples to find. There will be one mark for each appropriate choice.

'Explain' asks the student to say what impact or effect the writer is hoping to have on the reader. There will be one further mark for each clear explanation.

Question 4

This is a 'How' question. Questions that start in this way are asking the student to focus on the way the writer uses devices to create an impact on the reader. In this case it is about presentational devices. Students must do more than 'spot' devices. They are expected to explain how devices are used deliberately by the writer to have an impact on the reader.

Question 5

Another 'How' question. This time the focus is the use of language.

Question 6

'Compare' questions ask students to explain what is similar and what is different about two texts. Make the point that the candidate will always be given a particular focus. In this case, it is presentational devices. Remind students of the language that is used in comparison. You might suggest connectives like: similarly ... in the same way ... whereas ... like ... on the other hand ...

Working through the lesson

Activity 1 The pair work will promote discussion of the question type and as well as the required extraction of details and discussion of devices. When complete, the teacher may want to allow students time to compare their ideas with another pair. Whole class discussion should be avoided as it will affect the later activities.

Worksheet 11a may be useful for students to record their notes.

Sample answers

🔑 Write and assess activity: Understanding non-fiction texts 1

🔑 On your marks activity: Understanding non-fiction texts 2

🔑 Write and assess activity: Understanding non-fiction texts 3

Students here are being made aware of the way a mark scheme works. Checking their own answers will allow the students to identify their strengths and areas for development. Take feedback from the students on questions 1–4 and then you may want to ask students what they found easy and what they need to work on. Then you could keep a record to inform your future teaching.

Activity 2 Before the students begin Activity 2, highlight the point that while students make a lot of points about the text, they are mainly explaining what they see rather than commenting on the effect of the presentation/organisation on the reader. Focus on the examiner's comment. Ask the students to think about:

- The amount of text compared to presentational features like pictures. How is the balance of text and pictures likely to affect the readers' desire to read it? Why?

- Who is the text aimed at? What kind of people? Is it likely to appeal to them? Why?

- What is the overall impact of the whole page? Is it appealing? Why/Why not?

When the class has discussed their answers to these questions, you could ask the students to work in pairs to complete the activity. You could then take feedback from the pairs and ask them to read out one of their sentences and ask the class to comment on whether it addresses the examiner's concerns. Worksheet 11b accompanies this activity.

Activity 3 This activity may be carried out in several steps.

Step 1

Read through the question and the explanation of the question's requirements and the specimen answer (up to the Activity box).

At this point, you should introduce the table featured below: explain how it encourages the student to find examples and then to think about the focus of the question, that is, how the language creates interest and informs the reader. Explain how the modelled answer shows the impact of the language on the reader. Now ask the class to complete the table, making notes on the impact of the language on the reader.

Question 5: The Boys Are Back in Town
How does the writer use language to interest and inform the reader?
(8 marks)

Examples of language used	How it is used to interest or inform
Language to interest • Repeated use of the second pronoun 'you'. • Use of adjectives, e.g. 'enchanted, crinkle-cut', 'smooth green grazing lands'. • Comparison with 'the children's first sight of Never Never Land in Peter Pan'.	• Involves the reader. Makes it more personal. Makes it easier to imagine, as if the reader is there.

| **Language to inform**
 • Details of what you see from the plane, e.g. 'The coves, and bays and beaches', 'Pathways zigzag up and down the gulleys'.
 • Facts such as 'two thousand miles from any other city' and 'over the horizon there's Sydney'. | |

Step 2

Direct the class to address the tasks in the Activity box.

Step 3

Ask the students to work in pairs to compare answers.

Step 4

After students have attempted Activity 3 and discussed their answers in pairs, take feedback. It may be useful to ask any pairs who feel they have done well to read out an answer and to explain why it is a good one. You could then ask for constructive comments from the class. Sometimes students who are finding this question difficult may be prepared to read their answers and ask for help from the class. Discussions of this type ensure that students focus on the assessment criteria.

Activity 4 This activity is staged so that the security of discussing with a partner will allow students to focus on the requirements of the question. Worksheet 11c accompanies this activity.

Question 6
Choose two of these items which use presentational devices.
Compare the ways presentational devices are used in them in order to interest the reader.
(8 marks)

Again, there are several steps you could follow to engage students with this activity.

Step 1

Read the textbook entry for question 6 up to the Activity box. Remind students that comparison questions require them to make judgements/give opinions. They need to comment on devices that work well or fail to work. Make the point that the examiner is less concerned with the opinion than with the way the student uses evidence and explanation to support her/his viewpoint.

Introducing the table may help the students by making comparison easier. The criteria for the judgement/opinion are in the first column. The students can read across the table when they have completed the next two columns. This will make it easy to spot similarities and differences. The second row is where the students can record their opinions and reasons. You could show this to the class, ask for a presentational device from one of the texts and then show the class how to write up and support an opinion about the impact of that device.

	Text 1	Text 2	Similarities and differences
Presentational devices used			
How successful they are in appealing to the reader			

Step 2

Ask the students to complete the table in pairs and then try to write an answer.

Step 3

After the answers have been written, return to the whole class forum and mark some responses together. Highlight:

- points made
- comments that explain how interesting the presentational devices make the piece appear to the reader
- the language of comparison.

You could use different colours to do this and use the visual impact to show how well students have completed each element of the question or to point out areas for development.

Now ask the students, in pairs, to carry out the same highlighting activity with their own answers.

Plenary

Having looked at a whole reading section, students will now have a clearer picture of the aspects of the examination process that they are comfortable with, and aspects they find challenging. The teacher should ask the students to list aspects of the examination paper they feel they understand and those aspects on which they need more help. They could do this in pairs. Take feedback and keep a record of what the students say. Use this to inform future planning of examination lessons. Students respond well when subsequent lessons are based on the feedback they have given.

Outcomes

In this chapter your students have:

- learnt and understood the layout and format of the exam question paper
- learnt and understood the question types
- learnt and understood the marking schemes and how they are applied
- participated in reflective paired discussion about exam format and marking
- assessed their own performance and identified areas for improvement.

12 Making your reading skills count in the controlled assessment

AO focus

English AO2 Reading and English Language AO3 Studying written language.

- Read and understand texts, selecting material appropriate to purpose, collating from different sources and making comparisons and cross-references as appropriate.

- Develop and sustain interpretations of writers' ideas and perspectives.

- Explain and evaluate how writers use linguistic, grammatical, structural and presentational features to achieve effects and engage and influence the reader.

- [English AO2 only] Understand texts in their social, cultural and historical contexts.

In this chapter your students will:

- learn more about how their reading skills are tested in the controlled assessment

- explore the different choices available to them

- look at sample tasks and answers and consider how they can improve their answers.

Additional resources

Worksheet

12a: Sample tasks and answers

Working through the chapter

The reading requirements are different in the two specifications below.

GCSE English

Students need to respond to:

- a play by Shakespeare

- a prose text from either a different culture or the English Literary heritage

- a poetry text from either a different culture or the English Literary heritage

Students will explore each of these texts by responding to the same task. They will produce three separate responses, one for each text. For example, the task may invite students to explore the characterisation of the central character of the text, or to explore a theme like family relationships or the relationship between man and nature. The same task will apply to each text.

GCSE English Language

Students need to respond to one 'extended text'. A text consists of:

- a novel

- a collection of 7 short stories

- a play

- a collection of 15 poems

- a literary non-fiction text (e.g. biography or travel writing)

Students will have a choice of tasks from which they choose one. In this specification students will have up to 4 hours of controlled assessment time to be spent on one text whereas in GCSE English the same amount of time is devoted to three texts, suggesting that in GCSE English Language the response will be more wide-ranging in the way a single text is explored.

What is controlled assessment?

You may have a class of students who are all taking the same specification which will make it relatively straightforward to explain the single set of requirements. If you are dealing with a situation in which you have students who are being entered for different specifications or who might in the future be entered for different specifications then it would be sensible to focus on the similarities, the common features:

- basically the same AOs
- the same amount of time
- similar tasks
- the same ground rules for preparation and then undertaking the controlled assessment.

GCSE English

There is one Assessment Objective which applies only to GCSE English: 'understand texts in their social, cultural and historical contexts.' There is no requirement for this AO to be applied to all three texts in the controlled assessment, but it must feature somewhere.

The best way to approach these contexts is to begin with the text being studied. If, for example, the literary heritage text being studied is *Oliver Twist,* the most sensible way to find out how society and culture were different in Dickens's time is to explore the novel. Students will achieve nothing by including potted biographies of Charles Dickens or hugely generalised information about life in Victorian England. By generalising, about the position of women in society, for example, students present a very stereotypical, bland view of an era they may know little about.

The key point about the contexts is that any response to them needs to be relevant to the task in hand. If, for example, the task was to explore 'family relationships' in a text like *Romeo and Juliet* it would be best to begin with the family relationships in the play. Exploring the relationship between Capulet and Juliet would lead most students to the realisation that social values have changed over the centuries. Far better to respond to this than to introduce some ideas about Elizabethan values which are likely to be over-generalised.

The same approach would be necessary in the response to a text from a different culture. The best way to find out about American culture and society in the 1930s as it applies to *Of Mice and Men* is to explore the text. That might lead to some light historical research, but any observations must be rooted in the text.

The ground rules about the actual controlled assessment task are quite straightforward but those concerning the planning, preparatory stage need to be clearly explained:

- 'notes' must not constitute a pre-prepared draft
- students must keep a scrupulous record of any resources they use to help them prepare
- the teacher is not allowed to comment on a prepared draft and give feedback before the controlled assessment.

It is worthwhile drawing the attention of students to the advice about selecting important parts of a text for analysis. Notes should include some form of list of the sections of text which are going to form the basis of the student's response.

Introducing the tasks

Foundation tier students should be familiar with the ideas of theme and character.

Characterisation and voice

This is largely straightforward but it might be a good idea to draw attention to the difference between character and characterisation. The focus should be on characterisation, i.e. the ways in which a character is created, developed and used by a writer. The key AO is:

- Explain and evaluate how writers use linguistic, grammatical, structural and presentational features to achieve effects and engage and influence the reader.

The focus is clearly on the techniques used by writers to 'achieve effects and engage and influence the reader.' Writing about characters as though they are real people is something that students very easily slip into and they need to be shown the correct focus at an early stage.

Themes and ideas

This may be more difficult idea for some students. It would be a good idea to identify a literary text which the group now study and to invite responses to a question about what the main themes or ideas are.

The Reading AOs are explained in Chapters 11 and 12 of the Student Book because not all of them are applicable to the exam. It would be useful to have student-friendly versions of the AOs on display for constant reference together with students' work annotated to exemplify different Assessment Objectives. It would be difficult to work though all the AOs in a lesson with a class: it is, for example, quite difficult to grasp the implications of the AO concerning the contexts without a concrete example. It is far more helpful to students, especially those entered for the Foundation Tier, if they work on the AOs discretely.

Some aspects of the AOs will need careful teaching for Foundation tier students. For many of these students developing their ideas presents difficulties as does the explanation and evaluation of writers' use of linguistic, structural and presentational features.

Sample tasks and sample answers

[k!] Learning activity: Extended reading on poetry

[k!] On yours marks activity: Extended reading on 'themes'

[k!] Planning activity: Extended reading response

You may only have to focus on one of the specification panels in the Student Book. If you do have to address, though the panels should make it fairly straightforward to see a great deal of common ground.

The information in these panels should lead to some discussion of time-management. There are significant differences between the two specifications because in one, students have to write about three texts and in the other it is only one text, but the same amount of time is allocated. It is very important in the case of GCSE English that students realise they have about one hour to write about a text and that as they prepare their notes they have the limitations of time firmly in their sights.

Because there is choice of texts, it is impossible to provide activities covering the three areas required for English – drama, prose and poetry covering Shakespeare, English Literary Heritage, and different cultures. The example is based on poetry from the English Literary Heritage and focuses on a potential theme.

The poem 'Below the Green Corrie' (Text A) is taken from the *AQA Anthology*. Annotated copies of texts may not be taken into controlled assessment but working on the annotation of a clean text has obvious benefits at the preparation and planning stage.

It would be useful to students to discuss the annotations on 'Below the Green Corrie' as a whole class, perhaps with the annotated version of the text on an interactive white board. This would enable students to practise the skill of explaining and evaluating writers' use of linguistic features. Some students may need revision of the term

'simile' and all would benefit from a discussion of the implications of the simile 'like a bandit'. You may wish to explore with students what they thought the mountains had done to make the life of the poet 'enriched.' Further useful discussion could be carried out around the oxymoron in line 6 'marvellous prowlers'.

In order to enable students to focus on an aspect of the text, you could examine the description of the 'leader' at the beginning and end of the poem.

The timings in the plan are very rough guidelines but, given the timing restrictions of controlled assessment it would be worthwhile discussing timings and planning for them in the preparation stage. For students working at Foundation Tier it is good practice to ask them to identify quotations before they begin a task to ensure that they make appropriate references to texts.

Activities 1 and 2 It would be helpful to elicit students' responses to the two passages (Text B and Text C) before they read the teacher's comments. They will all identify the better response but it would be helpful to tease out explicitly the elements of the second response which make it better – mainly the way ideas are 'sustained and developed'. One way of showing this would be to look at what is written about 'bandits' in each response.

Activity 3 In Activity 3 students are asked to make improvements to a student's response on Text D, the poem 'Storm in the Black Forest' by D.H. Lawrence.

You may want to read through the poems as a class and highlight some of the following details from the table below and Text E – the student response – before asking students to suggest improvements.

Example from the text	Annotation
'bronzey soft sky'	Suggests the writer sees beauty in nature – the repetition of the 's' sounds opens the poem in a gentle tone.
'jugfull after jugfull of pure white liquid fire, bright white'	Describing the sheet lightning as liquid, using the commonplace 'jugfull', removes any sense of fear; it is an unusual but quite gentle image.
'gold-bronze flutters'	The colours again suggest beauty and the word 'flutters' is a soft, gentle word.
'sometimes / a still brighter white snake wriggles among it, spilled / and tumbling wriggling down the sky'	The introduction of 'snake' to describe the forked lightning introduces a potentially more menacing tone but that is balanced by the almost playful sense of the repeated 'wriggles', 'wriggling'.

Example from the text	Annotation
'the heavens cackle with uncouth sounds'	There is a suggestion of the supernatural here as 'cackle' suggests witchcraft. 'Uncouth' suggests wildness, lack of civility.
electricity	Introduces an element of science – a shift in the poem from a romantic portrayal of the power of nature to a scientific interpretation of what lightning is.
'is supposed to have mastered / chained, subjugated to his use!'	The use of three variations on the idea of enslaving, alongside the repeated 'supposed to' reveals the writer's main idea which seems to concern the beautiful power of nature which is beyond the control of man and science.

The table below contains the comments which students should be guided into making about the response to the poem, Text E. You could begin by allowing the students to discuss the text and comment on it with a partner before a whole class discussion.

Once you have discussed these with students you may wish to ask them to write their own response to the task.

Text E	Possible advice
The writer begins by describing the lightning.	This is not accurate. The writer begins by describing the sky. The student has missed an opportunity here to comment on the description in the opening line 'the bronzey soft sky'.

He makes it seem very bright and white.	The student should have followed this statement up with a quotation such as 'jugfull after jugfull of pure white liquid fire'. Following comments could have drawn attention to the repetition in this line as well as the implied admiration of the beauty of the lightning.
He says the lightning is like liquid and like a wriggling snake.	There is no attempt here to comment on the choice of images for the lightning, nor to examine the positive and negative aspects which are presented here.
This makes me think he doesn't like the lightning…. I think this makes him angry.	The student shows some awareness of the focus of the title, the poet's relationship with nature but clearly this needs a much more detailed explanation with reasons for the anger and dislike being explored.
I think he wishes man could have better control over the weather.	This is certainly focused on the key element of the task and reveals some understanding of the central idea of the poem but the student misses an opportunity to explore the effect of the repetition in the final lines, misses the impact of the exclamation marks.

Outcomes

In this chapter your students have:

- learned about how their reading skills are tested in the controlled assessment
- learned more about the ways they can achieve high marks in this part of the course.

Section B: Writing

Overview

Section B of the Student Book is designed to develop students' skills in writing as defined by the Assessment Objectives for GCSE English (AO3 Writing) and GCSE English Language (AO4 Writing) and tested in the exam and the controlled assessments.

GCSE English: AO3 Writing

GCSE English Language: AO4 Writing

- Write [to communicate] clearly, effectively and imaginatively, using and adapting forms and selecting vocabulary appropriate to task and purpose in ways that engage the reader.

- Organise information and ideas into structured and sequenced sentences, paragraphs and whole texts, using a variety of linguistic and structural features to support cohesion and overall coherence.

- Use a range of sentence structures for clarity, purpose and effect, with accurate punctuation and spelling.

The chapters provide opportunities for students to draw on and revise the skills they have already acquired in writing, and to develop these further. The learning objectives, founded in the Assessment Objectives but in 'student-friendly' language, are given at the start of each chapter. Throughout each chapter the learning points are clarified and modelled, and followed by activities for students that are designed to reinforce and extend their learning.

Students are encouraged to work independently in pairs or small groups, as appropriate, and are given regular opportunities to assess their personal progress and that of other students, often against fixed criteria. The learning within the chapters is cumulative, building on what has come before, and at the end of several chapters there is a summative activity which challenges students to demonstrate their learning across the whole section.

Each chapter can be used as a discrete stand-alone topic with activities and tasks specific to the named objectives. They do not have to be done in the order in which they appear in the Student Book, though it is worth noting that this order was arrived at after careful consideration of how best to build students' skills in writing.

Assessment

GCSE English	GCSE English Language
External exam: Writing non-fiction texts (1 hour)	**External exam:** Writing non-fiction texts (1 hour)
Controlled assessment: Producing creative texts (up to 4 hours)	**Controlled assessment:** Creative writing (up to 4 hours)

Nelson Thornes resources

Chapter	Student Book activities	kerboodle! resources
13: Communicate clearly	1: Identifying verbs and subjects in sentences 2: Using capital letters and full stops correctly 3: Rewriting dialogue using correct punctuation 4: Using alternative forms of punctuation to commas and adding punctuation to make a paragraph clearer 5: Matching tenses of verbs 6: Re-writing and extract using past and then present tense Check your learning: Writing an extract from your own life story using sentences, correct punctuation and different verb tenses Stretch yourself: Using the same skills to write a short section of a biography	● Worksheet 13a: Verb and subject ● Worksheet 13b: Punctuation 1 ● Worksheet 13c: Punctuation 2 ● Worksheet 13d: Writing a review ● Worksheet 13e: Correct tenses ● Text transformer activity: Writing accurately ● Learning activity: Practising punctuation ● Learning activity: Matching tenses
14: Say what you mean	1: Identifying the purpose of a text; writing text that could be used to persuade people to buy something 2: Identifying the audience of a text 3: Writing sentences that could be used to appeal to a particular audience 4: Identifying purpose, audience and language features in a range of texts 5: Writing texts for different purposes and audiences using appropriate language features 6: Exploring the purpose of text messages and explaining how texting can be used 7: Writing an informal email 8: Identifying ways in which a formal email differs from an informal email ; writing a formal email 9: Identifying the features of a formal letter Check your learning: Writing a formal email or letter for purpose and audience using appropriate language, organisation, tone and form	● Worksheet 14a: Who is the audience of a text? ● Worksheet 14b: Informal and formal emails ● Worksheet 14c: Formal letter to complain ● Learning activity: Using language for different audiences and purposes ● Learning activity: Formality and informality ● Analysis activity: Comparing formality ● Analysis activity: Identifying forms
15: Building paragraphs	1: Organising ideas into a logical sequence 2: Pair discussion of different ways to plan a piece of writing 3: Using one of the planning methods to plan a section of an autobiography 4: Ordering the paragraphs in a text 5: Putting paragraphs into a text 6: Developing longer paragraphs by adding details Check your learning: Pair or group review of key learning points	● Worksheet 15a: Organising autobiographical information ● Worksheet 15b: Sequencing and organising ● Worksheet 15c: Organising ideas into a whole text ● Write and assess activity: Organising your writing ● Analysis activity: How texts hang together ● Learning activity: Organising writing ● Learning activity: Organising information
16: Word play	1: Thinking of different ways to group words 2–3: Experimenting with synonyms 4: Identifying verbs and adjectives in sentences 5: Forming an impression of a character based on details from a text 6: Writing descriptions of different characters 7: Analysing how writers choose vocabulary for different audiences Check your learning: Rewriting a student's sample answer to make it more interesting for a teenage reader Stretch yourself: Writing about a favourite subject at school in an interesting way for a specific audience	● Worksheet 16a: What is vocabulary? 1 ● Worksheet 16b: What is vocabulary? 2 ● Worksheet 16c: How can word choice change meaning? ● Worksheet 16d: Choosing vocabulary for audience and purpose ● Worksheet 16e: Engage your audience ● Learning activity: understanding vocabulary choice ● Learning activity: Choosing vocabulary ● Learning activity: Vocabulary choices ● Text transformer activity: Selecting vocabulary 1 ● Text transformer activity: Selecting vocabulary 2

Chapter	Student Book activities	kerboodle! resources
17: Different sentences	1–2: Recapping verbs and subjects and how they are used 3: Identifying the use of connectives in compound sentences 4: Identifying main and subordinate clauses in compound sentences; rewriting compound sentences 5: Examining the effects of using different types of sentence structures 6–7: Rewriting simple sentences as complex sentences 8: Matching annotations to highlights in a text to understand how writers use different sentence structures for effect Check your learning: Writing a first-person narrative using a range of sentence structures	• Worksheet 17a: Writing compound and complex sentences • Worksheet 17b: Check your learning: 'Child Soldiers' • Learning activity: Simple sentences • Text transformer activity: Combining sentences • Learning activity: Sentences and clauses • Connecting comments activity: Sentences in action
18: Writing non-fiction	1: Sorting fiction and non-fiction texts 2: Examining the structure of a newspaper article 3: Writing a newspaper article based on a factual paragraph, to engage readers; peer assessment of articles 4: Identifying how writers make links within and between paragraphs 5–6: Planning and writing a newspaper article Check your learning: Analysing and writing an editorial	• Worksheet 18a: Text types • Worksheet 18b: Newspaper articles • Worksheet 18c: Newspaper story commission • Worksheet 18d: Check your learning • Learning activity: Non-fiction texts • Planning activity: Informative writing • Planning activity: Persuasive writing
19: Writing fiction	1: Pair discussion of childhood stories 2: Making notes on a childhood event 3: Identifying techniques used to develop characters in a script; continuing a script 4: Writing a continuation of a script using similar dialogue style to the author 5: Identifying key features of writing prose 6: Continuing a prose narrative 7: Analysing techniques used by poets to create characters; writing one stanza of a poem about an imaginary friend 8: Practising a controlled assessment-type task in either prose, drama or poetry Check your learning: Peer assessment of the written response to Activity 8	• Worksheet 19a: Choosing what you know • Worksheet 19b: Writing for yourself • Learning activity: Exploring creative forms • Planning activity: Writing from experience • Connecting comments activity: Writing fictional texts • Write and assess activity: Writing creatively
20: Adapting forms	Review and reflect: Recapping audience and purpose 1: Rewriting text for a different audience and in a different form 2: Writing a short informative text 3: Writing the opening text for a website aimed at young people; peer assessment of writing Check your learning: Writing a commentary on the response to Activity 3	• Worksheet 20a: Audience and purpose quiz • Learning activity: Linking vocabulary, effect and audience • Learning activity: Making information exciting • Learning activity: Writing short responses to non-fiction texts • Analysis activity: Understanding and writing reviews
21: Genres	1: Pair/group discussion of music and film genres 2: Using clues about the setting to identify the genre of a text 3: Using clues about the setting to identify the genre of a text, re-writing opening sentences in a different genre 4: Identifying aspects of a text that create tension and suggest genre 5: Writing a continuation paragraph from a choice of genre extracts keeping to the same style 6: Identifying aspects of writing that add to tension 7: Writing in two different genres using a photograph as the starting point 8: Changing the form of a text but keeping the key features of the genre 9: Writing a short story based on an opening line in either the science-fiction or detective thriller genre Check your learning: Recapping key features of different genres	• Worksheet 21a: What is 'genre'? • Worksheet 21b: Identifying genre 1 • Worksheet 21c: Identifying genre 2 • Worksheet 21d: Genres of texts • Worksheet 21e: Features of a text 1 • Worksheet 21f: Features of a text 2 • Worksheet 21g: Using a photograph as a basis for writing • Worksheet 21h: Features of a text 3 • Worksheet 21i: Writing in a specific genre • Learning activity: The features of genre • Learning activity: Setting and genre • Planning activity: Writing for genres • Connecting comments activity: Writing in genre

Chapter	Student Book activities	kerboodle! resources
22: Making your writing skills count in the exam	1: Identifying audience and purpose for two exam-style questions 2: Re-drafting a sample answer based on examiner's comments or writing a letter asking for a part-time job 3: Improving a sample answer to an example longer writing task Check your learning: Reviewing the learning from the chapter	• Worksheet 22a: Questions for discussion • Worksheet 22b: Student responses to exam questions • Planning activity: Organising your ideas • On your marks activity: Analysing a Writing answer
23: Making your writing skills count in the controlled assessment	1: Looking at a 'Moving images' task and how to write about the way that atmosphere is developed in a film 2: Experimenting with a poem as the for a 'Prompts and recreations' tasks 3: Planning a response to a 'Me. Myself. I.' tasks and writing the opening paragraph 4: Writing a response to a commissions task Check your learning: Reviewing the learning from the chapter	• On your marks activity: 'Moving images' task • Video case study activity: 'Moving images' video • Connecting comments activity: Changing texts for a 'Re-creations' task • On your marks activity: 'Re-creations' task • On your marks activity: 'Commissions' task

Student checklist worksheet

Read through the following list of skills which you will be expected to show in your Writing work for GCSE English or GCSE English Language.

Rate your own skills using the columns as a tick chart and then check out which chapters might be most suited to help you tackle any areas you are not sure about.

Skill	Very confident	Quite confident	Sometimes I can't	Often I can't	Which chapters might help?
Know what a sentence is					13, 17
Write in sentences					13, 14, 17
Use a range of sentences					14, 17, 18, 20
Use a range of punctuation					13, 20
Understand verb tenses					13
Organise into paragraphs					15, 18
Plan before writing					15, 18, 20, 21
Use varied words					15, 16, 17, 20
Write for a purpose					14, 16, 18
Write for an audience					14, 16, 17, 18, 20
Choose words for effect					16, 17, 20, 21
Write fiction					16, 21
Write non-fiction					14, 15, 18, 20

Use your responses to the checklist to set yourself *no more than* three targets to achieve from the Writing section.

1...

2...

3...

Checking students' progress

The tasks below are all included in the Student Book and can be used to check student progress in a particular skill.

Chapter	AO focus	Activity from Student Book and learning outcomes
13, 17	• Write to communicate clearly. • Use a range of sentence structures for clarity, purpose and effect.	**Chapter 13, Check your learning** Students: • write an account of an event that has had an impact on their life • create a plan for their writing • make notes on their chosen event • write in sentences • use correct punctuation and grammar • use correct verb tenses. **Chapter 17, Check your learning d)** Students: • vary their choice of simple, complex and compound sentences when responding to the task • use a range of openings to sentences to engage and interest the reader. **Practice** **Punctuation revision**: Use enlarged punctuation marks on individual sheets. Provide explanations on alternate sheets. Challenge students to find the correct pairings. **Speech punctuation**: Write unpunctuated sentences on a whiteboard and invite students to punctuate using coloured pens for different forms of punctuation. Discuss whether correct or not with group. **Sentence openings**: Provide additional words for more able students and encourage them to experiment with alternative structures/sentence starters. Encourage use of appropriate punctuation.
14, 20	• Use and adapt forms appropriate to task and purpose to engage the reader.	**Chapter 14, Activity 3** Students: • write a formal letter of complaint about a bad experience in a restaurant • consider purpose, audience, content, organisation, language, tone and form. **Chapter 20, Activity 3** Students: • use information from an advertisement image to write 5 short paragraphs for a web page aimed at young people • use personal pronouns • choose appropriate vocabulary to engage their readers • use a range of sentence structures • use a range of punctuation correctly. **Stretch yourself** • Extend understanding by providing other types of text and inviting students to suggest suitable purposes and audiences for each one. This could be done as a quiz. • Extend students by challenging them to change the audience for their text but still use only 50 words to describe it. Potential audiences could be teenagers or retired people. Encourage students to think about suitable attractions as well as language variety.

Chapter	AO focus	Activity from Student Book and learning outcomes
15, 18, 19	• Organise information and ideas into structured and sequenced sentences. • Organise information and ideas into coherent paragraphs. • Use a variety of linguistic features to support cohesion and overall coherence.	**Chapter 15, Activity 4** **Students:** • rearrange paragraphs of recipe instructions to make a content sequence. **Chapter 18, Check your learning** **Students:** • write five paragraphs for an editorial • use appropriate linguistic features and vocabulary to support their argument • use a range of sentence structures to have an impact on their reader and to support their argument. **Chapter 19, Activity 8** **Students:** • create a clear plan including the order of their piece of writing • use a range of techniques to structure their fiction writing • write in an appropriate form • organise their writing and use sentences and paragraphs as appropriate • use appropriate linguistic features to create settings, character, situations. **Practice** **Key word knowledge:** Check student understanding of keywords (highlighted in orange) by playing a 'Call Your Bluff'-type game. Teams of students should invent two false meanings and one correct for three selected key words and then challenge another team to spot the correct one. **Sequencing:** Invite students to extend their skills by writing instructions for a skill they can teach to another student. In pairs, each one should read their instructions and see how well the other can learn what to do. Use a recent story from a tabloid paper, enlarged and cut into paragraphs. Invite students to reassemble the story in the correct order using contextual clues. **Newspaper story:** Remind students of marking criteria – sentence variety and paragraphs being essential. Refer to punctuation work done in Chapter 13 and a third of marks being linked to this. **Editorial writing:** Students could prepare a speech on a topic about which they feel strongly. This could be delivered to the group before formulating as an article.
16	• Select vocabulary appropriate to purpose and audience.	**Chapter 16, Practice** **Writing for effect:** Students explain feelings about place first, while others suggest appropriate vocabulary. Students use suggestions as basis for writing before sharing. Visual learners may benefit from having an actual image to focus their ideas on when writing information about animals.
21	• Use and adapt form, style and language to a wide range of genres.	**Chapter 21, Activity 8** **Students:** • write a short story of 5–6 paragraphs • create a plan for their short story • select vocabulary appropriate to their chosen genre • use dialogue correctly where relevant • link the story to the opening sentence provided. **Practice** **Writing for a genre:** Ask students to provide their own images and then select two different genres to describe what they see in different ways. Use the resultant writing as part of a display to exemplify different genres.

General resources

The resources in the Student Book, Teacher's Book and *kerboodle!* provide a range of learning opportunities for students and give them practice at developing their skills using a wide variety of text types. The resources suggested below can be used to reinforce, develop and extend students' skills and learning further.

Types of resources	Author and title
Autobiography – extracts from autobiographies by celebrities are often useful.	• David Beckham: *David Beckham: My Side* • Jade Goody: *Forever in my Heart* • Peter Kay: *The Sound of Laughter*
Short stories – extracts from the short stories in the *AQA Anthology* may be useful for practice in identifying varied sentences and the effects created.	• Haruki Murakami: 'On Seeing the 100% Perfect Girl One Beautiful Morning' • Elizabeth Baines: 'Compass and Torch' • Penelope Lively: 'The Darkness Out There' • Helen Dunmore: 'My Polish Teacher's Tie' • Clare Wigfall: 'When the Wasps Drowned' • Leila Aboulela: 'Something Old, Something New' • Ridjal Noor: 'Anil'
Additional texts used in Section B.	• Willy Russell: *Blood Brothers* and *Our Day Out* • J Priestley: *An Inspector Calls*
Preparation texts for the extended writing tasks – some of these may provide useful themes, such as: children, crime and punishment, families and friendship. These may also offer additional extension reading for students wanting to improve their independent comprehension skills.	• Robert Swindells: *Stone Cold* and *Heroes* • Phillip Pullman: *The Amber Spyglass* • Susan Cooper: *The Dark is Rising* series
Films/DVDs	• *Van Helsing* starring Hugh Jackman (2004). Watching the extract referred to in the review in Chapter 13 may enable students to better understand the sequence of events, before attempting to rewrite it. • *Harvey* starring James Stewart (1950). This film gives an old-fashioned take on the idea of an imaginary friend, except the character who 'sees' it is an adult and the 'friend' is a huge rabbit. This film may provide stimulus for discussion linked with *Brendon Gallacher* in Chapter 19: Writing fiction. • *Brideshead Revisited* starring Jeremy Irons (1981). Extracts from the film showing the house and grounds may be useful for students to use ideas for their written descriptions. The original series is also available to download at: http://www.itv.com/ClassicTVshows/perioddrama/bridesheadrevisted/default.html
Useful websites	• Most newspapers have a website on which it is possible to find recent news stories. Students could use research skills to locate other animal stories and images to provide further practice in using tabloid paragraphing. Some that may be useful include: www.dailymail.co.uk; www.timesonline.co.uk • For students with low literacy levels or special educational needs, it may be useful to use www.firstnews.co.uk

13 Communicate clearly

AO focus

English AO3 Writing and English Language AO4 Writing

Write [to communicate] clearly, effectively and imaginatively in ways that engage the reader.

In this chapter your students will:

- practise making their writing clear to a reader
- revise using correct sentences, punctuation and verb tenses.

Additional resources

Worksheets

13a: Verb and subject

13b: Punctuation 1

13c: Punctuation 2

13d: Correct tenses

13e: Editing a review

Getting started

Revise knowledge of verbs and subjects in sentences. Prepare cards using sticky labels with either a past tense verb or a noun; some could be proper nouns. As students arrive in the room, give each student one card. Explain that the purpose of the lesson is to improve understanding of communicating in sentences. Ask students with verbs to stand up (remind them what a verb is if necessary – a doing or being word). Instruct them to choose a partner who is holding a noun. The students should discuss whether the words they are holding form a sentence or not. Encourage the students to explain their reasoning. Try to help students understand that though sentences can be structured similarly, unless the words make sense, it is not a sentence.

Working through the chapter

What makes a sentence a sentence?

Text transformer activity: Writing accurately

Activity 1 This is a reinforcement and revision activity which may benefit students of all abilities. It may be appropriate to remind students that a third of marks may be allocated to punctuation

and sentence structure. Worksheet 13a may be used with this activity.

Answers			
Sentence number	Verbs	Nouns	Real/not real sentence
1	ran	dogs	real
2	swim	mobiles	not real
3	swarmed	police/estate	real
4	swooped	computers/chairs	not real
5	dives	milk/ice	not real
6	was	tea/table	real

Encourage students to use the examples as models if they are not sure about how to make sentences that are not really sentences. Refer back to the Starter activity to reinforce what is needed to make a sentence.

Using punctuation to make sentences clear

Learning activity: Practising punctuation

This section deals with punctuation ranging from the basic essential components to direct speech.

Move the focus on to punctuation. This is an area that is often overlooked by students, but it is important for both GCSE and Functional English, so it is worth ensuring students revise this thoroughly.

Activity 2 Encourage students to read the passage and try to make sense of it before starting to draft it with capital letters and full stops.

a

Answers
The cup match started at three o'clock. Both teams had been training hard for weeks and wanted to win. The fans were keen to see the trophy won by their team. This match was the most important of the season

b It may be appropriate to use Worksheet 13b to support the matching activity. This could be made more suitable for kinaesthetic learners by students cutting the columns up and matching them by sticking onto another piece of paper.

Activity 3 Reinforce the importance of correct speech punctuation. Remind students that speech marks only go around the words being spoken. Students may benefit from being able to experiment with correctly punctuating the passage on a small whiteboard before committing it to paper. Worksheet 13c accompanies this activity.

Answers

"What time does the show start tonight?" asked Jenna.

"I think it's about seven, but it might be later," replied Sara.

"Seven? I can't be ready by then."

"You'll have to try!" snapped Sara though she knew she was wasting her breath. Jenna couldn't ever be ready on time.

Students could revise their skills by continuing this written conversation, correctly punctuated.

Stretch yourself
This activity at the bottom of the worksheet could be used as a research task for more able students.

Why are commas not enough?

Students who are uncertain about sentences often use 'comma splicing' as a way to avoid having to finish a sentence with a stop. Encourage students to work in pairs and attempt to read Text A on 'Van Helsing'. Direct them to pay particular attention to the punctuation; that is, not taking a breath until there is a full stop. They may then be able to explain the difficulties presented by constant use of commas.

Activity 4 This activity 4 uses Text B. Worksheet 13d may be suitable to support this activity.

Visual learners may prefer to use a range of colours and lines or arrows to assist them in planning their improvements. Ensure students understand that editing is a necessary process in improving work, and should not simply consist of copying out work more neatly. For controlled assessment tests and Functional Skills, students will benefit from knowing how to edit work by looking at punctuation and altering vocabulary to make the whole text more interesting to read. Support could be directed to assisting students with sorting out the information into a more logical sequence before trying to rewrite the text. It may be helpful to cut Text B into sections and

place linked ideas together in order to see how an alternate structure could be created.

Using the right verb tense

k! Learning activity: Matching tenses

Consistent use of tenses can be another major factor which students find difficult. Creating a 'Word wall' of verbs in their different forms for the different tenses may offer students a straightforward way to check their own consistency as they write.

Activity 5 Check that students understand the concept of tenses. Ask individual students to say one sentence about something they did last week (so using the past tense), for example, 'I went to the cinema'; followed by a sentence explaining what they are doing now, for example, 'I am sitting in an English lesson'; then a last sentence saying what they are going to do at some point in the future, for example, 'Next week I will be on holiday'.

Alternatively, to make the learning more kinaesthetic, ask students to write one sentence in the tense of their choice. Then, have the entire group reorganise themselves into three smaller groups around the three verb tenses. Students should check other members of the same group to make sure everyone is in the right place. Those incorrectly grouped should be helped to understand why they need to be in a different tense. This should be done before the task which involves the rewritten texts.

Activity 6 This activity uses Text C. Worksheet 13e may be used here.

a   Challenge students to correctly identify the verb participle and match it with the appropriate forms of the verb. Make it more challenging by inviting students to write a sentence on a whiteboard, with the tense on the back. Students could show the board to their peers and challenge them to identify the tense correctly. This provides checking for all students as those showing the sentences also have to be correct.

b   Students may find it useful to identify the different tense of the verbs first and then carry out the rewriting tasks. Refer students to the exercise done first if they become unsure about the ways the tense can be formed to provide a little variety.

Check your learning Some students may find this a challenging task, for personal reasons as opposed to literacy difficulties. Try to be sensitive to this and be prepared to offer the extension task instead if it becomes clear that it is too distressing for them to complete an autobiography.

It may be useful to expand students' understanding of autobiography and biography by providing a range of texts or text extracts to look at. Students who are unlikely to tackle the extension task or undertake to carry out independent reading may enjoy having short sections to look at that are written by or about well-known figures.

Encourage students to plan their writing before choosing an event from their life to write about. The suggested strategies for planning are the most common ones but students may have their own ideas. It may be useful to offer 'sticky notes' for students to record memories and then sequence them without having to rewrite notes.

It may be advisable to encourage students to share some of their ideas around the class, in small groups or in pairs before they start writing. Model how to ask suitable questions by inviting a student to share an account to which you respond. Some students may benefit from being able to bring in a photo or object from home to assist them with focus on the event. ICT may also offer some students the opportunity to experiment with sequencing and checking of tenses.

Encourage peer feedback and assessment by reminding students of the expectations of the task relating to sentences, punctuation and tenses.

Stretch yourself

More able students may enjoy the challenge of writing a biography about someone they admire. This could be someone in their own family rather than a celebrity. The task will also offer opportunities for using research skills and creative writing skills, as well as providing a recap on the use of punctuation and sentences.

Challenge students who are working on this task to read some biographies to gain some awareness of the different styles.

Suggested reading

Lewis Hamilton: *Champion of the World – The Biography* by Frank Worrall.

David Tennant: *A Life in Time and Space* by Nigel Goodall.

Michelle Obama: *Michelle Obama* by Sarah Parvis.

Sir Alan Sugar: *Sir Alan Sugar: The Biography* by Charlie Burden.

Plenary

If you feel confident of the ability level in the group then you may want to suggest an interactive plenary. Provide A4 paper for each student (this can be scrap but needs to be clean enough to write on) and ask them to make a paper aeroplane. Divide the class into two teams and instruct them to stand on either side of the room with a pen and their aeroplane. Each student should write onto the plane one thing they have learnt from this unit about sentences. On instruction, planes are thrown across the room to the other team. Invite individuals to read some of the comments aloud, then get them to add another comment on the topic of punctuation. Again, these should be thrown towards the opposite team. Again, invite some comments to be read aloud before adding a final comment about what has been learnt about verbs and tenses, and throwing it again across to the other team.

The activity is intended to be a 'fun' reminder of the chapter aims plus provide kinaesthetic learners with an active way of recalling details.

Discuss with students which Personal Learning and Thinking Skills they have used during their work on this chapter. Encourage explanation of why they have chosen that particular area and which parts of their learning addressed it.

Outcomes

In this chapter your students have:

- revised their knowledge about sentences and word order
- been actively involved in punctuating and editing texts
- improved their awareness of the importance of verb tenses through class discussion
- taken part in reflective paired discussion about autobiographical episode
- given and received peer assessment of written tasks.

14 Say what you mean

AO focus

English AO3 Writing and English Language AO4 Writing

Write [to communicate] clearly, effectively and imaginatively, using and adapting forms appropriate to task and purpose in ways that engage the reader.

In this chapter your students will:

- learn how to write for purpose and for audience
- practise writing using different forms
- try using formal and informal writing styles.

Worksheets

14a: Who is the audience of a text?

14b: Informal and formal emails

14c: Formal letter to complain

Getting started

Explain that students are going to be creative thinkers for part of the lesson, and that they will use other aspects of Personal Learning and Thinking Skills in later parts. It should be expected that students are able to identify what other competences they are using as the lesson progresses.

Introduce the notion of things having a purpose by collecting a group of commonplace objects, for example a tin opener, whisk, bicycle pump, mobile phone, tissues (or pictures of them if actual objects are not feasible).

Allow students a few minutes thinking time while they look at these and then ask them to suggest ways that they are linked. This will encourage creative ideas and develop thinking skills as well as providing an introduction to the focus of the lesson. Discuss any reasonable links and ideas. Ask students to consider if the objects are interchangeable. Draw from these discussions the point that many things have only one main purpose and that it is not possible to use them as substitutes for each other. Link this point with texts. Suggest that, unlike objects, texts can have more than one useful reason for existing.

Working through the chapter

What is the purpose of a text?

Who is the audience of a text?

This section focuses on helping students understand that purposes can be identified through examination of the words and phrases used.

Ensure students understand the idea of text having a purpose and that a text can have more than one purpose. The examples provide structured guidance to assist students in identifying different purposes for texts.

Direct students to read through the example of the Fire Procedures and discuss the reason it has been written. Ensure students understand there is only one main purpose. Look at the other examples of purposes in the list and invite students to suggest what sort of writing would have those purposes (for example, adverts, health leaflets, books, magazines, directions, holiday brochure).

Stretch yourself

As an extension activity, some students could use alternate examples of texts available – this could be something brought in from home or texts around the school/room. Direct students to record their ideas as a reference for revision. Encourage discussion about different purposes and enable students to accept that there may be a range of purposes in a single text.

Activity 1

a Refer to the chocolate bar wrapper (Text A) and point out that one of the reasons people may have identified different purposes is linked with the probability that the text has different audiences. It is likely different people will be interested in the texts: parents may be interested in the nutritional information or someone with an allergy may want to know about the ingredients.

b Students should use the information gathered in a) to write the text for their chosen product. Remind students that they should focus on the purpose 'to persuade' when writing their text. They should also consider the audience they are trying to persuade for the particular product they have chosen.

c Students should compare their texts with peers and try to identify why one may be more persuasive than another.

d Follow on from the discussions by repeating b) for another product and using ideas generated by peers about what makes a text persuasive.

Who is the audience for a text?

This section provides a range of texts and challenges students to consider who may be appropriate audiences for them. Encourage students to understand that audience, in its widest sense, can be anyone who listens to, watches or reads something.

Activity 2

a The cartoon is written for a child audience. Discuss the language level, appearance and content of the story.

b The 'Milkodrops' recipe is of more interest to parents, or to teenager/adults who might buy the product for themselves. The writer probably had in mind a health-conscious parent, or an adult/teenager checking whether they are allergic to any of the ingredients.

Encourage students to stick to the word limit imposed. It may be useful for support to be directed to assist with collating a range of suitable words to use for the target audience (that is, adults) before students start to write the text.

Use a mini-plenary at this point to check that students have been able to carry out the writing activity successfully. It may be appropriate to invite students to read their persuasive texts aloud and encourage peers to comment on them, evaluating how well it meets the criteria. Ask which PLTS this activity addresses and discuss responses.

Activity 3

a It is important that the students understand that the words and content they use should be different for each audience (for example, simpler for children but providing nutritional facts for parents). When writing the 50 word advertisement (part c), students should focus on being persuasive, using the features of the sweets that would appeal to parents (for example, emphasising that they are sugar free).

Activity 4

🔵 Learning activity: Using language for different audiences and purposes

Activity 4 uses Texts C–F.

Encourage students to work in pairs through the different texts and discuss the different purposes and audiences for each one. There may be a variety of answers, which could all be correct. Students can be encouraged as creative thinkers to justify their views as much as possible. It may be appropriate to use Worksheet 14a to support the recording of the text types. The sentence completion exercise at the end of this worksheet provides support for students who may benefit from structured guidance when looking at details. A range of ideas is possible so accept reasonable answers to the purpose/audience sections.

Activity 5 Students should use the examples of a postcard (Text C) and a music review (Text E) in Activity 4 to model the sentence structure and type of comments to use. They should carefully consider the audience in each case.

Stretch yourself

The more able students could be provided with additional texts and instructed to add those to their table, completing ideas in each of the three columns. Suitable texts may include:

● a DIY manual

● the 'blurb' on the back of a book

● an extract from the textbook of another subject, for example, geography or science.

Take feedback on how these differ from the examples provided.

Choosing the right sort of language

🔵 Learning activity: Formality and informality

🔵 Analysis activity: Comparing formality

This section introduces the notion of language being chosen that is appropriate to purpose and audience, so it is important that students are confident with the above activities before commencing this.

Texting

Though it is important that students recognise text as a valid form of communication, it should be made clear that for exam and controlled assessment purposes text language is not generally thought to be acceptable.

Discuss with students how text messages are a relatively new form of communication and how quickly it has developed into its own unique form of writing. Use the annotated text message in the Student Book to discuss common features. You could ask students to type on their mobile an example of a text they would send to various people. Then you could transcribe it onto the overhead projector or whiteboard and analyse it in the same way to show them their own use of the features and that not everyone texts in exactly the same way.

Activity 6 It is likely that the students know just as much, if not more, about text messages than the teacher! The first parts of the question (a and b) may be successful as a whole class activity, particularly to include less able students in discussion. Some students may have had experience of teaching their mum or their granddad to text, so invite them to use this experience in part c.

Emails: informal

As more employers move towards 'paperless' offices, it may be useful to discuss with students why emails are now so useful in business and work placements. Discuss situations where emails are most commonly used and why. You may like to discuss advantages and disadvantages of emails.

Activity 7

a   Encourage students to respond to the informal email (Text H) equally informally. It may be necessary to ensure students understand that this form is not the same as using text-speak and should generally be in full words.

b   Students could annotate their email to highlight the same kind of features as were picked out in the example.

Emails: formal

Activity 8

a   Encourage students to look at the different ways language and tone have been used in the second email (Text I).

b   Worksheet 14b may be suitable to support this activity for students who are comfortable working independently. Other students may benefit from working with a member of staff to complete the sheet.

Formal letters

(kt) Analysis activity: Identifying forms

This section is intended to assist students in understanding that letter writing is possibly a format that may be assessed in the exam and that certain features of the letter would be expected by an examiner.

The situations given are intended as an opening for discussion. There may be disagreements over whether a certain situation requires formal or informal language, which would present the perfect opportunity to question students on their opinion and get them to think about *why* they think a formal/informal response would be more suitable.

Activity 9

Answers	
1	b
2	g
3	d
4	a
5	e
6	f
7	c

Explain that the letter (Text J) is structured in a clear and logical way, with a specific purpose to each paragraph. Display the letter using an overhead projector or interactive whiteboard. As a class, match each paragraph of the letter to one of the purposes listed below. Students' opinions may differ from these suggestions; if so, accept any answers that can be backed up with evidence.

Answers	
Paragraph 1	Opens with introductory explanation for writing
Paragraph 2	Describes how money was saved
Paragraph 3	Gives more details about what the problem was
Paragraph 4	Concludes with statement that shows the company is expected to do something.

Check your learning

Worksheet 14c accompanies this activity. Students could be directed to look back over the chapter before starting to write. Remind them that formal letters are polite and making threats or insults should not be part of what they are writing. They should use the Text J in Activity 9 as a model for their own writing. Encourage peer assessment and invite them to check each other's work and comment on it to help improve their writing.

Plenary

It can be useful to pause during the course of work and review what has already been learnt. Conclude by referring back to the aims of the chapter, plus the different Personal Learning and Thinking Skills that have been addressed through the activities that have been carried out.

Then ask students to prepare three points about writing for purpose and audience that they have learnt in this chapter, to share with other students. Some students may benefit from the opportunity to present this in different forms, depending on their preferred learning style. For example, it could be presented as a poster, delivered orally in a presentation or as part of Assessment for Learning when discussion about tasks is invited prior to redrafting, or as part of the final assessment.

Outcomes

In this chapter your students have:

- identified the purposes and audience for different texts
- commented on aspects of structure: vocabulary, sentences and punctuation in various texts
- actively participated in paired role play, adapting language to suit purpose and audience
- understood the differing forms of appropriate communication for different purposes and audiences.

15 Building paragraphs

AO focus

English AO3 Writing and English Language AO4 Writing

Organise information and ideas into structured and sequenced sentences and paragraphs.

In this chapter your students will:

- learn about ways to organise their writing using sentences and paragraphs
- make sure that what they have written makes sense to their reader.

Additional resources

Worksheets

15a: Organising autobiographical information

15b: Sequencing and organising

15c: Organising ideas in a whole text

Getting started

What does 'organised' mean to you?

Write and assess activity: Organising your writing

This section is intended to assist students in making explicit links between their skills in life generally and their skills in English. Understanding that they have such transferable skills may boost their confidence. It may also be worth making the link between skills learnt at school and those needed in work as being able to organise tasks or time independently are useful in both arenas.

Activity 1 The starter activity is focused on helping students to understand that in their everyday life, they already make choices about organising and sequencing to make things clearer or simpler.

The activity of sorting the list of chores into an acceptable sequence has no right or wrong answer. Students should be encouraged to discuss their choices/strategies and explain their reasoning. This will help to develop Thinking Skills as well as helping them to see that people generally organise things to their own advantage. Students should not be permitted to opt out of this by claiming they 'don't do chores' or similar. Point out that at work as well as home, decisions have to be made about the order in which to tackle jobs – if more appropriate (for example, with a mature group) suggest a range of work-based tasks instead.

Working through the chapter

Activity 2 The initial activities focus on prompting students to consider ways in which ideas can be organised and considering the appropriateness of some methods. Worksheet 15a accompanies this activity.

Encourage students to consider how things can be planned or organised using the examples of ways to plan and thinking about their suitability for the suggested tasks. It may assist students to decide on the suitability of the various methods if actual examples were available to examine/look at.

After the paired discussion, use a mini-plenary to bring out ideas from the class about how planning and organising can take place successfully. Invite contributions about how much time is spent planning and how useful methods may be. For controlled assessments, planning will be a useful skill and students may need this highlighted, perhaps linking with target grades and using comments from examiners/teachers.

Creating a plan

Planning is often regarded as something of an afterthought in exam situations. This section is intended to encourage students to see how planning can give them an advantage with longer writing tasks as it provides structure and a 'route' through the task. It may be useful to link the concept with the idea of planning a holiday or visit somewhere and considering what could be the result if no planning at all went into an excursion.

Activity 3 Remind students that purpose and audience are always important considerations when tackling writing tasks. Use the plans suggestions for practical ways that autobiographical writing could be planned. Students are encouraged to practise by using episodes from their own lives and then organising them using one of the outlined methods. At this point, students are not being asked to write an autobiography, but to consider how it may be structured.

How to sequence information

Analysis activity: How texts hang together

Learning activity: Organising writing

The example provided is a simple sequence. More able students may benefit from understanding that creative writing does not always have to follow a chronological sequence, but that some activities require it in order for the result to be correct.

Recap on the starter activity of reorganising the images and creating text to go with it. Ask students to speculate about what sense the text would make if the images were put back into their original order. Invite some students to read their text in that order to reinforce the fact that it will not make sense.

Activity 4 This activity uses Text A and worksheet 15b.

Go over the clues to sequencing information before allowing students to work on Text A: Making an omelette, in pairs. Kinaesthetic learners may prefer to cut the sentences up and rearrange them physically in order to determine the correct sequence.

Once finished, help students to see how the clues provided allow an appropriate sequence to be followed. Using coloured pens, ask students to link the ideas and words which provided the clues. For example, the connectives – words showing the process progressing, that is, 'chop onions' linked to 'chopped onions'. This could be modelled on an interactive whiteboard or enlarged photocopy. This linking process prepares students to start to see how texts are cohesive and have internal structure.

Stretch yourself

The activity can be extended by inviting students to create a similar sequence themselves for a relatively straightforward task, for example, making toast; downloading music onto an MP3 player or setting the alarm on their phone. Students could then cut the sequence up before passing to a partner to re-sort. Students should be encouraged to discuss the ease/difficulty with which they accomplished the task and to focus on the clues that were/were not provided.

For students who are kinaesthetic learners, the activity may be reinforced if they were able to carry out the instructions provided so that they could 'try out' how accurate their selected sequence actually was. This would need preparation, especially for activities like making toast.

How to organise ideas in a whole text

Organising writing into paragraphs is one-third of the marking criteria for exam and controlled assessment, so it is important that students have opportunities to revise this skill.

Paragraphs are an area that students may struggle to grasp. Provide some time for revision and revisiting to help overcome misunderstandings. Discuss any misconceptions, for example, that each paragraph should be a set number of lines long. It may be useful to create a reminder poster to put up in the classroom for students to refer to when working on tasks.

Activity 5 This activity uses Text B and worksheet 15c.

Students are going to look at a straightforward text (Text B) to see how it is sequenced and structured to make its message clear. This may be a suitable activity to model on an interactive whiteboard first. A worksheet with the text is available to use for annotation purposes. The symbol // has been used to show where a new paragraph should start. Students are asked to identify the reasons for the new paragraphs.

Stretch yourself

It may be appropriate to ask students to continue the story in a suitable way and to use two further paragraphs. These could be checked by another student to see if they agree about where the new paragraphs have been started.

Alternatively, students could check their ability to write in paragraphs by writing a short text about a holiday of their own and then sharing it with another student to see if paragraphs have been used appropriately. This will help to reinforce the skills practised.

Developing details in a paragraph

This section is intended to help students think about methods of improving their paragraph content and move on from simple 'tabloid' paragraphing.

🔲 Learning activity: Organising information

The 'exploded' text is intended to help students see how they can improve the quality of what they are writing through giving more detail. Work through the paragraph checking at each stage that students have understood the way the topic sentence is being developed. Ensure students understand 'anecdote' and that they are able to use second-hand (or even invented) stories to back up their points. Reassure students that making up statistics or anecdotes for exam purposes are quite acceptable as the examiners are marking their ability to write correctly, rather than looking for absolute truth!

Activity 6 Refer to Text C to remind students they have a model for how to develop a topic sentence. Students should pick the topic sentence about which they can think of ways to extend the point. They do not have to agree with it personally. Encourage students to work independently on the writing task in order to promote increasing confidence in their own skills before comparing with another student.

Weaker students may struggle to write about something with which they do not agree, so support could be used to help record ideas about the chosen topic sentence before starting to write the paragraph. More able students may be confident enough to continue the idea into another paragraph, perhaps offering an alternate view or adding another aspect to the point provided.

Check your learning Compare the results from Activity 6 through peer assessment. Provide the criteria from AQA related to Writing tasks and encourage students to discuss the extent to which their partner has been successful in addressing the three components. (The criteria can be found in Chapter 22 of this book). Share ideas for improvement.

Consider which aspects of Personal Learning and Thinking Skills have been addressed through the activities in this chapter.

Plenary

It may be appropriate for students to be in small groups to discuss the plenary questions and arrive at a group consensus of what has been learnt through this chapter. Alternatively, students could share ideas with the whole group so that a wider range of opinions is offered and heard. This may benefit aural learners.

Provide reminders of the work done in this chapter by asking different groups to focus on one question only. Their responses and ideas could be the basis for a short class presentation to answer the question, or they could create a visual reminder in the form of a poster.

Outcomes

In this chapter your students have learned how to:

- sequence ideas, lists and information in various ways according to purpose
- planned writing tasks in alternate methods
- shared ideas with peers, offering opinions and advice
- experimented with writing for a particular purpose.

AO focus

English AO3 Writing and English Language AO4 Writing

Write [to communicate] clearly, effectively and imaginatively, selecting vocabulary appropriate to task and purpose in ways that engage the reader.

In this chapter your students will:

● experiment with using different description words in their writing

● write texts for specific purposes and audiences.

Additional resources

Worksheets

16a: What is vocabulary? 1

16b: What is vocabulary? 2

16c: How can word choice change meaning?

16d: Choosing vocabulary for audience and purpose

16e: Engage your audience

Getting started

What is vocabulary?

Activity 1

(k!) Learning activity: Understanding vocabulary choice

Worksheet 16a accompanies this activity. Students rearrange the words given according to the subject area with which they mostly closely associate them. Reassure them that they may expect some to fit into more than one area. Students should compare ideas and discuss differences in the ways they have categorised the words. Discuss with the whole group how a word like 'mat' can also be affected by being used in a compound word such as 'doormat' or 'placemat' and the different meanings introduced by those. Go on to consider what this shows about the flexibility of the English language. Introduce the concept of context as having an impact on the meanings of words.

Alternatively, as students arrive, give each one a sticky label with a different subject area written on it, for example, geography or maths. This may need to be specific to your school so that students are familiar with the subject areas studied. Try to arrange it so that there are five to six students in each group. This could be done entirely randomly

or planned to provide mixed ability groups. Students should be seated with others who share the same subject label. Allow five minutes for each group to come up with a list of subject specific words on paper. Exchange the papers between the groups and instruct students to now remove from the list any words which could be used by another subject area, that is, they are not exclusive to that topic.

This should result in very few words being left, those that are may well be specialist terms or names of chemicals. Discuss with the whole group, before introducing the notion of 'context' and its impact on the meaning of words.

Activity 2 Worksheet 16b can be used to support this activity.

This links with Activity 1 and encourages students to play with words to alter their meanings by changing the context in which each one is being used.

Working through the chapter

How can word choice change meaning?

(k!) Learning activity: Choosing vocabulary

This section is intended to encourage students to experiment with words used and understand that greater variety in vocabulary will probably enable them to achieve higher marks in assessments.

It may help students who are kinaesthetic learners to actually act out moving in the different ways listed (walk, stroll, amble and stride). Invite students to demonstrate how each word represents a different way to move and allow their peers to comment. Extend the activity by inviting other students to suggest further words which are synonyms of 'walk' and having the volunteers adapt their movement to show the new words.

This type of activity could also be used for the next section, but modelled by the teacher. Speak to the class in each of the ways indicated so that students who are unsure of the gradations of meaning are enabled to hear and see how the different verbs affect the understanding of what is going on.

Encourage students to work through Activity 3 in pairs and share their ideas. It may be appropriate to discuss their understanding before moving on.

Activity 3 Using synonyms can help students to improve their writing as they avoid repeating the same words. Help students to understand that different words that have very similar meanings can be used effectively to show ability to vary vocabulary. The exercise has no right answers, but is intended to encourage students to discuss differences in meanings suggested by picking alternate words.

Revision of spelling of adverbs may be included at this point. Many students mistakenly use 'ley' at the ends of adverbs. Provide examples of wrongly and correctly spelt adverbs and invite students to identify the wrong spellings with an explanation of what is wrong with the word. Explicit learning of these spellings for a test may also assist in ensuring students learn the suffix correctly.

Activity 4 Worksheet 16c can be used to support this activity.

a   Refer students to the text box which explains what each type of word is. If using the worksheet, visual learners will be helped by being able to use different colours for each word type.

b   Students should have had examples of appropriate synonyms in an earlier activity. Remind students of the physical nature of the exercise done to demonstrate each word.

c   Students with literacy difficulties may benefit from being given a range of choices in each word category in order to help with developing the sentences into some that are more interesting.

Share the students' ideas and encourage individuals to read their sentences aloud.

Choosing words for effect

Students sometimes find the notion of 'effect' quite difficult. It may be useful to liken the choice of words to the choice of music or lighting in films. The director chooses what the desired effect on an audience watching will be and then establishes the best way to create that through loud/soft/fast/slow music or bright/subdued lighting. Explain that writers may set out to create similar feelings in a reader.

Remind students of the necessity of considering audience and purpose when writing. In addition, point out that experimenting with words makes it possible to adapt writing to address those areas in a better way.

Activity 5 Activity 5 uses Texts A, B and C.

Using drawing assists students in realising what they have read and also supports more visual and kinaesthetic learners. Each drawing should show

distinct differences. If time is short, or students are unable to draw well enough, suggest that students look closely at the drawings provided and assess their accuracy compared with the written descriptions. The questions posed in the activity can still be addressed using the same drawings.

Activity 6 This extends the ideas used in Activity 5. Students should use the various descriptions of the old lady as models to write their own descriptions of both a sad and happy child. Compare results by sharing or reading aloud and commenting on successful strategies. Students with literacy problems may benefit from being able to have a selection of appropriate words to assist them.

Stretch yourself

More able students could write more than three sentences of description for each suggested child, or experiment with describing children in other moods – for example, angry, frightened or excited.

Choosing vocabulary for audience and purpose

🔣 Learning activity: Vocabulary choices

This section reinforces skills taught in previous chapters when purpose and audience for texts were considered. If suitable, it may support this section to have available a range of texts written for children and some written for adults about similar subjects. This would provide further examples of the text types being used and provide students with a wider range to consider.

Activity 7 Activity 7 uses Texts F and G. Worksheet 16d can be used to support this activity.

a   Students are encouraged to practise what they have learnt by identifying the features of each text which betrays its audience. Annotations similar to those in the earlier activity could be used on the worksheet.

b   The follow-up activity invites students to create their own texts for different audiences using some of the techniques they have just examined. Encourage students to pick an animal – real or imaginary – about which they can think of sufficient information to make the task feasible. Students could share their work in pairs or small groups and use peer assessment to comment on each other's work. Alternatively, students could read their texts aloud to the whole group and see if their peers are successful in identifying the different audiences for each text they have written. If they are not, the group should be invited to suggest ways in which the word choice could be altered to make it more appropriate to the chosen audience.

Check your learning

(k) Text transformer activity: Selecting vocabulary 1

(k) Text transformer activity: Selecting vocabulary 2

Worksheet 16e supports this activity. Read through the text with students and discuss why it is not likely to attract a reader. Points which may be raised could include: little to interest a reader; no real drama to the account; no use of descriptive words; no references to feelings or thought which would make it more personal. Ask students to identify the intended audience and discuss ways in which the text could be changed to address that specific group.

It may help students to have access to thesauri if their own vocabulary is limited. Though this will not be permitted in an exam situation or controlled assessment, it may assist students to appreciate the range of words that can be used and expand their vocabulary.

More able students could be extended by addressing a different audience with the same text and changing the words again. Peer assessment may be suitable here to assist students with understanding the impact on another reader.

Plenary

One of the following options may be suitable for a plenary session:

1 Invite students to comment on what they have learnt by experimenting with vocabulary in different ways. This could be recorded on Landscape-oriented A4 sheets (coloured paper would provide greater interest if available) as a single sentence reflecting the main point they have gained. These sheets could then be used to create a 'vocabulary choices' wall with the sheets laid out like bricks to provide a reminder of what has been done.

2 Invite students to say which Personal Learning and Thinking Skills has been used during the work on this chapter. Ask which activities have supported which part of the competences.

3 Ask students to suggest how the skills learnt with words could be applied in other subject areas. This will provide a link with the starter activity but also enable students to understand, again, the transferable nature of their skills.

Outcomes

In this chapter your students have:

- understood the effect of context on word meanings
- learnt that synonyms can be used to vary expression for interest
- experimented with alternative words to create particular effects in text
- participated in paired work to improve text through peer assessment and feedback
- learnt how to identify features of varying vocabulary for different audiences
- learnt how texts can be adapted to suit different audiences.

17 Different sentences

AO focus

English AO3 Writing and English Language AO4 Writing

- Organise information and ideas into structured and sequenced sentences.

- Use a range of sentence structures for clarity, purpose and effect.

In this chapter your students will:

- experiment with sentences of different types

- think about the effects that the sentence structures have on the reader.

Additional resources

Worksheets

17a: Writing compound and complex sentences

17b: Check your learning: 'Child Soldiers'

Getting started

This section is intended to support students in using their knowledge of sentences to experiment with constructing them in different ways, and assessing their likely impact.

Students have probably 'done' sentences quite frequently, so may need only a brief reminder of types of sentences and how they are structured. As a quick check up challenge students to play 'Just a minute' (speak for 60 seconds without hesitation, deviation or repetition) on the topic of what they know about sentences. Allow five/ six to try this game. Ask students what they know now that they had forgotten before doing the starter.

If in any doubt about the ability of some students to be able to move directly onto this type of work, it may be appropriate to recap on the basic structure by referring to Chapter 13.

A more visual way of revising sentences would be to write a range of verbs and subjects on the board or interactive whiteboard and ask a student to come up to link a verb with a subject. They could then challenge a peer to make up a sentence using the two ideas. The rest of the group could assess whether a proper sentence has been created and then say what type of sentence it is. Allow three or four students to try this before checking what is understood by what a sentence is.

Working through the chapter

Sentences

k! Learning activity: Simple sentences

k! Text transformer activity: Combining sentences

Activities 1–4

k! Learning activity: Sentence and clauses

- Simple sentences: Activities 1 and 2

Check that students are only using simple sentences as this can be harder than may be imagined. Students may need to recap on what a simple sentence contains before moving on to the next activity.

- Compound sentences: Activity 3

Again, check that suitable connectives have been used to construct the compound sentences. Students who have literacy difficulties may benefit from being provided with a list of words from which to pick.

- Complex sentences: Activity 4

Students may struggle with main and subordinate clauses. A more interactive way to reinforce this is to have some clauses, both main and subordinate, on separate pieces of paper for students to cut up or in text boxes on screen to move around. Students could experiment with putting the clauses in different places to see the effect and learn more about the way sentences can be constructed.

The tasks following each explanation in the Student Book are intended to assist students with recapping on their previous knowledge and extending their willingness to experiment with forms of sentences. They may be able to work through these activities at their own pace. It may help less confident writers to try out ideas on small whiteboards first.

A fun way to remind students of the different sentence types is to play a form of 'Consequences'. Explain that the object is to write sentences in the three formats that are outlined in the book, but they will also learn about them having to make sense. Provide students with pieces of A5 scrap paper. Instruct each student to write a simple sentence onto the top of the sheet and then to fold it over so the next person cannot see what has been written. These sheets should then be swapped round the class (for added entertainment, these could be 'scrunched' loosely into balls and thrown at each other!). The next person should write just a connective onto the sheet before folding again and moving round to the next person. The third person should write another simple sentence before folding over and moving the paper on again. The fourth person opens the sheet and reads it. Allow students to share some of the sentences thus created.

As a slightly harder activity along similar lines, students could write the first clause of a complex sentence (making sure it would not stand as a sentence alone) before moving the sheet round for adding the remainder. This could then be followed by compound sentence writing as above. The results are even less likely to make sense, but may provide an amusing reminder of structural rules. Additional practice is available in Worksheet 17a.

Using a range of sentence structures

Students sometimes struggle to vary sentence styles and openings, so this section is intended to develop their ability to do this. The experimentation with the changes to sentence structures shows students that adverbs (*sadly*), prepositions (*on ...*) or nouns (*Emma*) can be used to vary their openings.

It may be useful for students to see how writers use a range of sentences in books or articles. Using a similar idea to that in the Student Book, provide small groups of students with texts or extracts of different types of writing and allow about five minutes for them to examine what type of sentences each writer has used. This could be done with a tally chart. Invite feedback about what has been found and any conclusions students have come to about the writing style and whether they feel that certain points have been emphasised as suggested. Challenge the groups to write up to five more sentences in the style of the text extract and using similar types of sentences. Share these before moving on.

Activity 5 Discuss the ways that each sentence, though explaining broadly the same event, actually draws attention to different aspects. Invite students to try and explain the subtleties in difference. Challenge students to suggest other ways that sentences could be started, for example by using the verb first. Use ideas about a following sentence to discuss how each sentence prepares the reader for a slightly different continuation. This may be suitable to link with writing for purpose and audience addressed in other chapters.

Vary openings of sentences

Activity 6 Encourage students to be creative in the ways they turn the simple sentences into complex

ones by using the words provided. It may be useful to model how a similar sentence opener could be used to change the meaning in order for struggling students to have an example on which to base their own ideas. For example, write the words 'Often Emma ran away from home' and invite students to complete the sentence in a way that makes the phrase make sense. Replace the word 'Often' with another from the box and ask if the rest of the sentence still makes sense. Amend the original as necessary before inviting students to work on the others.

More able students may be able to suggest alternate ways of improving the original sentence and should be encouraged to try out any ideas they have. Peer feedback and comments may assist students in refining their sentences further. Paired discussion about any effects of the sentences may also help to remind students that they need to remember their audience when writing.

Sentences in action

Connecting comments activity: Sentences in action

The non-fiction text deals with an emotive topic. It may be necessary to be sensitive to students' personal experiences, particularly if cohorts include students from countries with a history of civil unrest and/or war. If it is felt unsuitable for students, it may be useful to refer to alternatives which nonetheless provide a range of sentence structures and will enable students to attempt a written response, though this will need to be planned in response to the chosen text. Some websites which may provide suitable material have been suggested in the additional resources section in the introduction to this section.

Give students the opportunity to respond to the experiences of the girl as recounted in Text A: Child soldiers. Then direct students to read the annotations to see how the writer uses sentence structure to make the message clear. Invite students to identify compound sentences and comment on how they have been used to provide a wide range of details about her experiences and build a fuller picture.

It may also be useful to draw attention to the annotations which refer to the use of vocabulary, for example, the repetition of 'she' to enhance the focus on the girl and reiterate the extent of her abuse; the repetition of 'children' to remind readers of the age of participants. Ask students to pick out how the writer has linked ideas through words selection – for example, violence, forcibly, beat, made to, abhorrent – all of which indicate the extreme situation she was in and the level of hostility she was subjected to.

Check your learning Students are offered the opportunity to carry out a piece of writing using the ideas read and discussed in Text A. The main purpose is to encourage thinking about the use of different sentence structures to create tension or express ideas in a certain way. Worksheet 17b is available to support this activity.

Stretch yourself

More independent learners could be invited to research the topic of child soldiers and present their findings to the rest of the group. Alternatively, it may be suitable to use the other suggested topics for students to identify a subject in which they have an interest. Invite them to write about an aspect of that – for example, animal testing, recycling, choices post-16 – in a way that helps inform other students. The emphasis should still be on using a range of sentence structures to create interest, and could still be shared with peers for editing advice.

Plenary

Refer back to the starter activity and opening tasks. Ask students to tell their partner one thing they have learnt about sentences from this chapter and how they have used this knowledge in their writing. Invite some students to share what their partner has told them. This provides reinforcement of the learning plus encourages auditory recall.

Outcomes

In this chapter your students have:

- explored a range of sentence structures
- explored a variety of openings of sentences
- learnt to write sentences in alternate formats
- learnt how to read a non-fiction text to identify ways the writer uses sentence structure
- learnt how to write in a role.

18 Writing non-fiction

AO focus

English AO2 Reading and AO3 Writing

English Language AO3 Studying written language and AO4 Writing

- Explain and evaluate how writers use linguistic features to achieve effects.
- Organise information and ideas into structured sequences.

In this chapter your students will learn how:

- texts are structured
- to organise information into texts
- to write non-fiction texts.

Additional resources

Worksheets

18a: Text types

18b: Newspaper articles

18c: Newspaper story commission

18d: Check your learning

Getting started

Introduce the topic by asking students to spend two minutes thinking of three reasons why planning a written task is a good idea. It may be suitable to explicitly link this with GCSE assignments and controlled assessments so students are thinking of the appropriate planning context. Invite students to share their three ideas with a partner and agree a combined list of three reasons. 'Snowball' this activity by asking the pairs to move into a group of four and again agree three reasons. Extend the discussions by moving again into groups of eight, if desired, and repeating the exercise of narrowing down. Select a speaker from each group to present the ideas to the whole class. Take feedback and ideas. Be prepared to accept creative suggestions, but remind students that the purpose is for planning in an exam.

Ensure students know that work in this chapter is intended to assist in developing their skills as writers of non-fiction texts.

Working through the chapter

Activity 1 Discuss/revise terms 'fiction' and 'non-fiction' before starting the activity. Allow time for discussion and selection of types. Worksheet 1 can be used for learners who prefer kinaesthetic activities. This task can be done as a class using an interactive whiteboard. Students should be familiar with the use of a Venn diagram from mathematics lessons, but be prepared to explain the principle behind it if students seem to be uncertain. Students may notice that there are more text types in the non-fiction list. Ask them to suggest reasons why that may be the case. There may be some debate over some types, for example, that not all poems are fiction – some are based on real-life experiences. Help students to see these discussions/ideas as part of the creative thinking process and a sign of an enquiring mind – even if no conclusions can be reached. Worksheet 18a may be used with this activity.

Newspaper articles

🕅 Learning activity: non-fiction texts

In this section students are encouraged to learn how newspaper articles are structured and to see how to use this in their own writing.

Students may be less familiar with the notion of a daily newspaper, as many households now access their news via the internet or TV. It may be useful to display some web pages from newspapers with examples of tabloid stories which are suitable for students to read before looking at the text provided. Students using the worksheet are provided with brief scaffolded sentences to assist them in formulating their ideas. The majority of the text types listed are non-fiction. This is to provide students with a range of writing examples in that type, but also because much of the reading done for work/college/entertainment after leaving school is based on non-fiction.

Read through the next section introducing the newspaper article and the questions answered by most articles. Look first at the 'basic' version of the story (Text A) and annotations to see how quickly these can be answered. Next, suggest students work in pairs to look at the actual text (Text B) and identify where the questions are addressed.

Activity 2 Activity 2 uses Text B. Worksheet 18b provides the text to annotate for this task.

Answers	
a	The verb 'roared' deliberately clashes with the notion of 'mouse' as they are not concepts that are usually linked.
b	The writer is playing on links between 'rules' and 'game', with 'tight spot'. Also the reference to 'cat' makes it sound less dangerous than it could have been for the mouse.
c	Accept any reasonable selection of striking words/phrases providing the student can justify their view.
d	Students should identify that the real version is more dramatic, but perhaps also that 'feeding' the reader with information gradually makes you want to read on to find out what happened.

Activity 3 Worksheet 18b provides the text to support this task.

Explain to students that they are going to try and construct a similar story about an animal using the five questions as a basis. Direct students into small groups and invite them to discuss how they would organise the information provided into a story about the baby hare. Students should be encouraged to try and stick to the facts provided, but to consider alternate ways of organising it. Students may benefit from being able to cut up the individual sentences and rearrange them to experiment with the structure. Encourage students to play with words to create a suitable headline, perhaps exploring possible puns or alliterations. This may need further explanation if students are literal learners who struggle to 'see' figures of speech. Examples of headlines which use these types of language devices may be needed to improve understanding of how they are used.

Students should have time to peer assess one another's work and share comments about the final story and structure in answer to the questions. There are no definitive answers, but students may comment on the differences that alternate sequencing makes.

Students need to be sure that they understand why and when paragraphs are used. The exercise as part of a pair should recap on that knowledge.

Check learning has been secured by suggesting students carry out a similar activity as a homework exercise. Provide an image on which students could base their story or invite students to locate their own to use from a newspaper or website.

Organising ideas

Planning activity: Informative writing

In this section students will learn how to improve the cohesion of text by varying words and phrases.

They will also look at how paragraphing can be used in different ways for different purposes. It may be useful to briefly recap on the reasons for beginning new paragraphs using the 'Background' box.

- New paragraphs are started when there is a change of time, change of speaker, change of location, change of topic.
- There is no minimum length for a paragraph, some can be a single word.
- Each paragraph should contain one main idea.

Activity 4 Read through the article about the Mako attack (Text C) and assist students in seeing the ways that the writer has structured the story. The annotations provide information about how this has been done. Direct students to complete the table in pairs.

Draw attention to the notion of 'tabloid' paragraphing which basically involves only one or two sentences per paragraph. Students may need assistance to improve their paragraphing away from this method. Explain that extended paragraphs are expected by both controlled assessment markers and examiner as these show ability to develop ideas beyond a simple structure.

Having worked on a range of stories and structures, students are asked to focus on using their knowledge to address a commission type task.

Activity 5 Students may need support to plan the details of their article. Worksheet 18c provides some prompts and questions to assist students in planning.

It may be useful to provide sticky note pads for students to write outline ideas and encourage them to move them into a suitable sequence before writing the whole text. Support may be directed to assist students with selection of details to include and planning the paragraphs before encouraging students to write the article itself.

Stretch yourself

Students who have coped well with this task could be invited to write another article about an unusual sighting of an animal. Provide only a basic outline of an idea – for example, a rare lizard is found in a box of bananas at a local supermarket – and challenge them to create a newspaper story around that. A similar structure to the one outlined could be used with appropriate quotes invented to go along with it.

Check your learning Worksheet 18d accompanies this activity.

(kt) Planning activity: Persuasive writing

The final section deals with editorial writing. It may be useful to supplement the material with actual texts from newspapers and/or magazines for students to read. This could be set as homework in an earlier session.

Organise the students into small groups to read through the editorial 'Pets are a health risk!' (Text D) and the annotations and share their responses. Check that students understand how the writer has structured the article to build up his points about having a pet. Draw attention to the varied paragraphs – some short and simple, with others that involve personal anecdotes and emotive comments.

Students may need support to identify a topic about which they feel strongly and can present a number of related points. It may be useful to offer a range of subjects suited to the group based on personal knowledge of their interests and inviting students to pick one.

Encourage peer assessment of the finished writing to provide students with immediate feedback about the effectiveness of their views.

Stretch yourself

Students who cope well with this task may be able to tackle writing an editorial which challenges the views of the one in the Student Book. Suggest that students try to write as a pet lover, arguing that having an animal is actually good for the well-being of the family. This offers opportunities for students to experiment with linking ideas on a theme in response to what they have read, rather than as something they believe.

The editorials produced, or extracts from them, as a result of these tasks may be suitable for display purposes. In that way students would have visual reminders of what they had achieved in this chapter, but also be able to review their learning as needed.

Alternative tasks in different writing styles which could be provided as practice for exams or as homework tasks are:

a   Imagine you are interested in a weekend job helping out at a local vet's surgery. Write a letter of application to the Practice Manager, explaining why you think you would be suitable for the job and what experience you have with animals. Remember to set it out as a letter.

b   Your local branch of the RSPCA is being threatened with closure due to lack of funds. Write an article for the newspaper explaining why people should be willing to support the work the organisation does by giving money. Try to include a range of persuasive points.

c   You have been invited to contribute to a radio documentary about people and animals. You are going to give information about caring for pets in a household with children. Write the presentation you will deliver. Remember that you will be giving the presentation out loud to an audience listening at home.

Plenary

Suggest that as a quick way of summing up the learning that has taken place, students try and set a question for someone else to answer which tests what they have learnt about writing non-fiction. Divide the class into two teams. Start the process by picking one student to challenge another on the other team to answer correctly. Award one point for correct answers. If the answer given is wrong, the unsuccessful team does not pose a question until answering successfully again.

Reward the 'winning' team by allowing them to leave the session first!

Outcomes

In this chapter your students have:

● understood the structure of newspaper articles

● responded to texts and images in writing

● worked as part of a pair/small group

● constructed articles based on factual information

● presented personal views in the form of an editorial.

AO focus

English AO2 Reading and AO3 Writing

English Language AO3 Studying written language and AO4 Writing

- Explain and evaluate how writers use linguistic and presentational features to achieve effects.
- Write [to communicate] clearly, effectively and imaginatively.
- Organise information and ideas into structured and sequenced sentences.

In this chapter your students will learn:

- more about how texts are structured
- to organise creative ideas into texts
- to write in different fiction formats.

Additional resources

Worksheets

19a: Choosing what you know

19b: Writing for yourself

Getting started

When students arrive provide them with one of the suggested story ideas from Worksheet 19a and explain that they will be telling a story based on the idea they have been given. This could be done by copying and cutting the worksheet so each student is given a slip of paper, or alternatively the worksheet could be enlarged and each student directed to sign their name next to the one they prefer as they enter. Each student will have a different suggestion for a story they can tell. Most students should be able to recall stories they heard or told themselves when younger, but the list also includes suggestions about personal anecdotes and recollections. Group the students into four or fives. Try to avoid friendship groups as the members may already know some of the stories about to be told and the challenge is to try and tell a story to people less well known.

Explain that each student will have only one minute to speak on their topic. In that time they must aim to get through the whole account but not speak so briefly that they are waiting for the time to end. Students should not be permitted to 'pass' on their turn, but encouraged to speak for

the full minute. You may wish to allow student to swap ideas if some have better accounts than others, but this needs to be at your discretion. Suggest students spend a couple of minutes thinking about what they are going to say before starting. Stress it can be a fictional account if they cannot think of a real-life story to tell. Keep a strict eye on the time and prompt the start and finish of the minute.

Take feedback from the class about:

- the constraints the time limit put on what they could say
- find out if anyone spoke too briefly – how that was perceived by the group
- discuss which speakers were regarded as successful and why.

It should be possible to link this exercise with the writing for controlled assessment and exam as:

- both will impose time limits
- the writing is on a specific topic rather than one of their own choosing
- an examiner will not know them at all so details need to be made explicit
- they will be expected to draw on some of their own experiences and knowledge.

Working through the chapter

Planning to be creative

In this section students will learn how to draw on their own knowledge as sources for ideas for creative writing.

This links to the starter activity in worksheet 19a.

Activity 1 Following the group activity, students are asked to work in pairs to share more detailed memories of stories. The questions are intended to focus their thoughts on the impact that fiction can have on lives, regardless of age or ability, and that even if reading is less popular now, films carry many of the fiction types only seen in books previously. If any student can recall a particularly strong response to a story in whatever format, it may be helpful to invite this to be shared with the whole class. Alternatively, it may be appropriate for staff to share similar recollections which may help students understand that even for adults, fiction can impact on thinking and feeling. (As an interesting aside, research indicates that people who read fiction develop a greater emotional resilience than those who do not.)

Choosing what you know

(k!) Learning activity: Exploring creative forms

(k!) Planning activity: Writing from experience

In this section students will learn about using their personal experiences as sources for creative writing.

Activity 2 Encourage students to share their memories of childhood, perhaps from primary school age, as a 'snapshot'. The questions are intended to act as prompts only, rather than to be answered specifically. If the non-fiction chapter has been covered, students may connect the questions being posed with the five basic questions which a newspaper article answers. This could be useful as a reinforcement tool and to make links between different writing genres. Worksheet 19a may be suitable to help students record their memories and impressions.

Writing script

In this section students will read a script and identify features of realistic dialogue. They will learn about using dialogue appropriate to the scene.

Students may be familiar with the layout of a script, but it may be useful to ask them to identify presentational differences between the *Blood Brothers* script extract (Text A) and prose. By referring to the annotations around the extract, points about the purpose of the writing can be drawn out, for example, that scripts are written to be heard or seen usually, rather than simply read.

Activity 3 This activity uses *Blood Brothers* by Willy Russell (Text A).

The extract from *Blood Brothers* is intended to demonstrate how dialogue can be used to show certain things about characters. Students could be invited to read this in pairs before answering the questions which follow in the activity.

Answers	
a	Russell uses short speeches with lots of questions, slang and colloquialism to show the ages of the speakers. What they do reflects youth – belief in blood brothers due to birthdays being the same, warning about it hurting when a knife is used.
b	Each character has a different use of vocabulary: Mickey uses slang and abbreviated words most, he calls his mother 'mam'; Edward speaks more Standard English, for example, references to mummy.
c	Students should be encouraged to think about realism and justify their responses to the question. An explanation of 'realistic' is provided in the Key terms box.

Activity 4 This activity uses Text A.

a Moving on, students are encouraged to discuss what else the boys may talk about – focus attention on typical things they may discuss: family, toys, games, pets etc. Working in pairs students should try to mimic the different dialogue styles used by each character for the next ten speeches. It may be useful for aural learners to try out the dialogue on each other before writing it down. Remind students to try and keep the lines short and use a childlike diction.

b These scenes should be shared between pairs and peer feedback given with comments based on success of meeting those criteria.

Writing prose

In this section students will learn about building up a sense of tension through giving a reader a few details at a time. They will also examine text to see how a writer gives a particular viewpoint.

Ensure that students understand the key words associated with prose writing. These will be useful for students responding to reading tasks as well as supporting their knowledge of how to address writing questions.

Activity 5 This activity uses 'When the Wasps Drowned' by Ciare Wigfall (Text B).

The extract also focuses on the presentation of children. The questions are very similar to those on the script in order to encourage students to make direct comparisons between the texts and understand that creative writing can use similar topics but present the material in quite different ways.

Answers:

a–b Wigfall shows they are children of different ages by showing them doing things that adults would not normally do. For example:

- Digging tunnels in the garden.
- Wearing a ring one has dug up.
- The younger one does not appear to question why she has found a ring in the soil.
- The older one is curious but not particularly worried.
- The way they speak is in short sentences. The younger one does not use proper sentences, for example, 'Found it'.

c Students may refer to the section highlighted in pink which refers to the state and size of the ring. They may also identify that the writer has made it sound quite cheap through using words like 'small' and 'thin'.

d Tension is built through the gradual unfolding of what is down the hole, with the final sentence being structured so that the 'pale hand' is mentioned almost at the very end.

e Students may pick out aspects such as:

- the reader has a better understanding of what the narrator is thinking and feeling

- readers only 'see' what the narrator explains so the account is one-sided

- readers realise the different ages of the characters through the protective way the narrator talks about her sister.

Activity 6

a Students should be encouraged to attempt the next two paragraphs independently before sharing their writing with a peer. Remind them that they need to continue using 'I' and 'we' when describing what happened next.

b Sharing their writing will enable students to see how different ideas can be developed. This may be appropriate for a mini-plenary where a range of different ideas are shared.

Writing poetry

In this section students learn how poetry differs from other forms of writing and experiment with writing a poem in the first person.

The final text used as stimulus for writing is the poem 'Brendon Gallacher' by Jackie Kay (Text C).

Direct students to read through the text several times and discuss what they believe to be the 'story' behind it. To develop a sense of exploration, ask students to present the story of the poem in a dramatic way. This could involve:

- dramatising the poem as a mime while someone narrates the text

- creating the 'story' which is the background to the extract

- producing a storyboard with captions to explain what has happened

- writing dialogue for the characters mentioned and reading them to the class.

It may be appropriate to differentiate the work by providing different groups with different tasks. For example, grouping the students by preferred learning style may facilitate different creative responses.

Allow time for students to work through their presentations and then invite them to present their ideas.

Take feedback from the rest of the class about ways that the story has been shown or developed. Ask them to consider how this type of work supports the creative writing process.

Activity 7

This activity a also uses Text C.

a–b Follow up the creative responses by focusing students more carefully on the text and addressing the questions. Remind students to also use the annotations to help find the answers.

c Some students may be able to draw on personal experience for their writing. Encourage them to share ideas if they are willing to do so, to assist students who struggle with imaginative writing.

Writing for yourself

🔟 Connecting comments activity: Writing fictional texts

In this section, students will learn about choosing appropriate tasks for controlled assessment and using their knowledge of different forms to achieve a successful result.

Activity 8

🔟 Writing and access activity: Writing creatively

The activities in the box are similar to those likely to be presented to students as part of their assessment. It is expected that students will select the form and task which they most prefer. Depending on the nature and make-up of the group, it may be more appropriate to direct students to focus on a particular option and work as a class to plan and write a response. In order to develop independent writing skills, it may then be suitable to set one of the other tasks as homework. Remind students about the warnings which follow each task and ensure they understand the assessment will be based on them responding in a suitable form.

The tasks themselves should be regarded as quite open-ended. It may be useful to direct any support towards students who may be entitled to Access Arrangements (using a scribe/ICT and/or reader is a skill which can be practised). Worksheet 19b may be used by students to record their writing.

Check your learning Students should be encouraged to peer assess each other's work and provide constructive feedback about what they have read. If possible, time for editing following that discussion could be provided and a further session of peer assessment given to consider ways that texts have been improved.

Plenary

Reflect on what has been learnt about writing fiction over the course of the chapter. Look back at the aims of the work and consider if these have been met. Students could be invited to spend a minute explaining to a partner the main thing they have learnt. Each partner could then move to another pair and change places. Each would then share the two things that each pair decided they had learnt. In this way students would hear four points about the learning from the chapter.

Outcomes

In this chapter your students have:

- understood that personal experience and knowledge are valid as a basis for creative writing
- read fiction in different forms and compared presentation of character and ideas
- produced written responses to stimulus in different forms
- worked as part of a pair and a group to present ideas and discuss topics
- used personal preferences to determine appropriate ways to respond to tasks
- revised conventions of fiction writing
- practiced for exam and controlled assessment.

20 Adapting forms

AO focus

English AO2 Reading and AO3 Writing

English Language AO3 Studying written language and AO4 Writing

- Read and understand texts making comparisons and cross-references as appropriate.
- Write [to communicate] clearly using and adapting forms and selecting vocabulary appropriate to task and purpose.

In this chapter your students will:

- learn more about how writers adapt their writing to suit purpose and audience
- think about how form affects writing
- experiment with language to create different texts
- ensure their writing suits their purpose and audience.

Additional resources

Worksheets

20a: Audience and purpose quiz

Getting started

Worksheet 20a may be used to support this Review and reflect activity.

Use the starter activity as an opportunity to revise earlier learning on purpose and audience and recap on any areas which are insecure.

When students arrive have the words 'purpose' and 'audience' displayed on interactive whiteboard or board. In pairs, ask students to spend three minutes discussing and writing down definitions for both words. This could be done using mini whiteboards. Take ideas from students and discuss differences in suggestions offered. It may be useful to link this with the quiz on the worksheet. Allow a further five minutes for completion of those questions before again checking answers and correcting any misunderstanding.

Answers for the 'Review and reflect' quiz	
1	b
2	d
3	a
4	d
5	d

Working through the chapter

 Learning activity: Linking vocabulary, effect and audience

Understanding audience and purpose of non-fiction writing

In this section students will learn how to identify different audiences and purposes using clues provided by the form and vocabulary used. The texts are all non-fiction as this is the genre most likely to be read and used after students have left school/college.

Text A leads directly on from the starter and provides reinforcement of skills as well as extending students to look more closely at text to identify differences in writing for different purpose and audiences. It may be useful to read the text and annotations with students and discuss any features which have not been highlighted but that students may think are significant. For example, the mention of the House being owned by the Queen's cousin is probably intended to suggest the importance of the place and show it has royal connections, which many tourists may find interesting. Likewise, naming the designers who were involved in creating the House and the varied range of different garden styles may interest different audiences altogether. Help students understand that the text is trying to appeal to a wide section of possible visitors.

Activity 1

 Learning activity: Making information exciting

a The website extract about Harewood House (Text A) has a specific audience and purpose. The annotations show the ways the writer has tried to make the text appeal to families. Students should use this text as a model to write their own version of a website entry for Alton Towers (Text B). Encourage students to follow the prompts to make the text more interesting to a reader. It may help students who struggle with writing tasks to make explicit the reasons why it is not very appealing. For example:

- the use of adjectives is not very imaginative
- the sentences are quite short and all quite similar in structure
- each sentence starts in quite similar ways which is boring and there are no words which 'grab' the imagination of a reader.

b Using coloured pens or pencils for the annotations will help provide visual reminders about the types of words used.

Students could be invited to write about a tourist attraction they have visited, for example, a theme park or castle. Their purpose and audience could be families again. Encourage them to use their personal feelings and experiences as sources for the comments made. This would also link with work done in Chapter 19, but provide a different genre to tackle.

Non-fiction travel guides

Invite students to compare the different ways the writers have provided information about Harewood House in Text A and Text C. This could be done by looking at the details identified in the annotations.

Students who experience difficulties with reading and auditory learners may benefit from hearing the texts read aloud before starting to discuss them.

 Learning activity: Writing short responses to non-fiction

Working in pairs, students should select five facts to use in their description. Students should be encouraged to consider which facts most suit their purpose and audience. It may need pointing out that different facts will be selected depending on these factors, but each different choice could be equally correct.

Stress that the word limit has to be adhered to. This is important in the controlled assessment tasks and students need to understand that some of their writing will be constrained by word limits. The facts are all written in note form already so it may be useful for students to think about why this may help them stick to the word limit. The editing process to reach the word limit is also useful as students may realise how much can be cut and yet still retain the sense of what they have written. Start students off on the process by suggesting words like 'the', 'and' and 'it' may not be necessary and encourage them to experiment with which words to remove – they can always be 'put back' if the remaining text does not make sense and other words then removed.

Though this section focuses on non-fiction writing, more able students may enjoy the challenge of trying out fiction writing with a similarly small word limit. Suggest they research 'mini-sagas' online or in a library. These are stories which have a moral or lesson for the reader, but which are restricted to exactly 50 words. Students may like to try this method of story-telling to further develop their skills. Competitions to find the best mini-sagas are held annually, so it may be appropriate to encourage entries from students who are successful with this genre.

Text D is also from a website, but with a different audience and purpose. Again the annotations will exemplify for students the way the writer has tried to appeal to a particular reader.

Analysis activity: Understanding and writing reviews

Examine Picture E and discuss what it shows. Encourage students to think about a range of reasons why young people may find it challenging or exciting to visit. Identify activities that may be possible there.

Students are expected to use their knowledge of purpose and audience, plus what they have learnt from Texts A–D to write their own web page about that specific attraction.

a   Ask students to pick out what their purpose and audience are to be before they start to write, to consolidate their understanding of the specific task. Again, encourage students to follow the prompts in order to ensure they structure the text appropriately and include the necessary details. They may also need reminding that the picture is a resource they can use for the details they need. Remind students that paragraphs are essential for gaining higher marks in both exam and controlled assessment. If they are uncertain about this, refer back to the work on paragraphs in earlier chapters as a quick reminder.

Students who have literacy difficulties may need support with selecting suitable vocabulary to describe the activities and to vary the sentences appropriately. It may be useful for sticky notes to be used for writing down ideas as these could then be moved about to choose the best structure.

It may be appropriate to set a time limit on this activity. Students will need to become familiar with working to a deadline. Allow perhaps 15 minutes for planning and the writing activity to be done. Provide warning of the end of the time for students who may have processing difficulties.

b   Sharing their texts provide feedback about the success of what has been written. Encourage discussion about how far students have met the criteria outlined earlier.

It may be appropriate to suggest a homework task based on writing about a local tourist attraction or well-known visitor centre. Students could carry this out independently to consolidate their skills and develop some confidence in their own abilities.

A specific purpose and audience could be set, or it could be left open to allow students to determine that for themselves and choose language and form appropriately.

Check your learning The writing of a commentary may not be a task which students are familiar with. Discuss reasons why this is a useful task to undertake:

- Ensures thought goes into what has been produced.

- Useful to try and think about the task after completion to identify ways it could be improved.

- Similar to evaluation in other subjects which informs students about strengths/weaknesses in process.

- Improves ability to carry out task on another occasion by reflecting on own learning.

Students could undertake this check independently before feeding ideas back to the rest of the group and comparing ideas.

Plenary

Return to the starter activity when students were asked to define what was meant by 'purpose' and 'audience'. Invite comments about those definitions and whether they would now change what was written in light of what has been learnt. Whether changes are made or not, select up to six students to explain their responses.

If available, students could use mini whiteboards to write one main idea they will retain about writing for different purposes and audiences. These could be recorded to put onto a revision mat for use later in the course, as part of their exam preparation.

Alternatively, as a change from students answering questions about their learning, ask students to write down an answer to a question linked with what has been learnt from this chapter. The challenge then is for their peers to think of a suitable question to go with it. This could be done in teams, for example boys versus girls or each side of the room to give a little competition.

Outcomes

In this chapter your students have:

- identified and explain 'purpose' and 'audience' for a range of texts

- used model texts to create their own writing

- understood how writers make their texts effective

- experimented with language for particular effects

- written texts in response to specific parameters

- peer assessed and evaluated work by other students

- reflected on learning undertaken during the chapter.

21 Genres

AO focus

English AO2 Reading and AO3 Writing

English Language AO3 Studying written language and AO4 Writing

- Read and understand texts making comparisons and cross references as appropriate.
- Explain and evaluate how writers use linguistic, grammatical, structural and presentational features.
- Write using and adapting forms and selecting vocabulary appropriate to task and purpose.

In this chapter your students will learn:

- to identify different genres
- prepare to use their ideas to complete a longer writing task.

Additional resources

Worksheets

21a: What is 'genre'?

21b: Identifying genre 1

21c: Identifying genre 2

21d: Genres of text

21e: Features of a text 1

21f: Features of a text 2

21g: Using photographs as a basis for writing

21h: Features of a text 3

21i: Writing in a specific genre

Getting started

What is genre?

From this chapter, students are expected to find out how to identify genres in texts and use some of the indicators in their own writing. However, it may be useful to link the concept of genre with other forms of media. The first activity focuses on music and film.

Select a range of music types and play a short extract from typical music tracks. Challenge the students to name the music style being played and to explain the features that make it that style rather than any other. It is likely if recent music is used they will be able to describe it as being created by a particular person/group who works

within that area; however, if less well-known music is chosen they will be obliged to listen and qualify their reasons more.

Draw out from discussions that individuals like different things in what they listen to because of their own preferences. Link this with what is watched on TV/films and also what may be read. Provide the word 'genre' on the interactive whiteboard or whiteboard. Link with the opening section in the Student Book that explains the meaning. Ensure students understand the term before moving on to the activities.

Working through the chapter

Activity 1 Worksheet 21a may be used with this activity.

a Students may be able to use some of the music types from the Starter activity to complete their list. It may be useful to suggest film titles for students who are unable to locate words for specific genres. This may then enable them to describe the type of film and decide upon a name for that style.

Text genres

Explicitly linking film genres with writing genres may help students understand the concept that writing can also be categorised in the same way. Check students understand the terms in the Key terms feature box in the Student Book. Lead on to explain that various features of writing can help a reader identify the genre from quite a short passage. The following activities could be worked through independently or as guided tasks.

Identifying genre

🔊 Learning activity: The features of genres

🔊 Learning activity: Setting and genre

Activity 2 This activity uses *Space Ranger* by Isaac Asimov (Text A), and Worksheet 21b.

Answers	
a	Science fiction (sci-fi) genre – refers to Martian, that is, from Mars, which is not a planet currently inhabited.
b	Accept any reasonable answers which may include: – summer referred to as being cold – could look directly at the sun – Martian desert has no vegetation.
c	The adjectives show the sun and sky to be very different to how they are seen from Earth. It sounds 'unreal'.

Activity 3 This activity uses *My Family and Other Animals* by Gerald Durrell (Text B), and Worksheet 21c.

Ensure students understand any unfamiliar words from the Glossary box.

Answers	
a	The texts are from different genres. The descriptions in each are markedly different. Text B is based in a different country; Text A is on a different planet.
b	Accept any reasonable answers about the effect of mentioning the plants and trees. Some may refer to the place sounding wild and out of control.
c	The rewriting exercise should focus on using words which give a more threatening impression to a reader. Invite students to share their ideas and evaluate who has created the most atmospheric opening.

Activity 4 This activity uses *In the Middle of the Night* by Robert Cormier (Text C), and Worksheet 21d.

Answers	
a	The genre could be regarded as thriller/horror – references to Hallowe'en and night reinforce this impression.
b	Accept reasonable accounts of why it is not an autobiography extract. These may include – mixture of tenses make the reader feel tense; the narrator is clearly recounting something which happens regularly.
c	The narrator uses words like restless, pacing, pretending she must call. These all give the reader the feeling of discomfort with events described.

Activity 5 By now, having looked at all three texts, students should be able to identify each genre and write a brief sentence about their reasons for thinking as they do. Accept justification for choices that are feasible.

The next texts explore how writers create a setting and atmosphere for a story. Students are invited to read the extracts and annotations to understand how words are used for specific effects.

Activity 6 Worksheet 21e has a copy of Text E, *The Grey King* by Susan Cooper for this activity.

Students are asked to apply their knowledge about how tension has been built and select details from Text E to annotate on their own. Support may be directed to assist with identifying words which sound threatening or unpleasant as aspects of tension.

Following responding to texts, students are invited to respond to an image. It may be useful to explain that it may be an image that is presented as part of the controlled assessment, so being able to experiment with writing in different ways could be a useful skill.

Activity 7 This activity uses Text F and Worksheet 21g.

This consolidates some of the skills already practised, such as swapping words to create a different impression of a place.

a It may be useful for less confident readers to make some notes about their response to the photo before beginning to write. This could be in the form of quick notes about what they can see, but looking at it from the perspectives of it being first pleasant and then threatening.

b Encourage students to think about ways to convey a happy, cheerful mood through the words chosen.

c The second version should be more unpleasant. Some students may simply replace some of the words with others that convey a different mood. Encourage more able students to experiment with changing sentence structure as well as words to give a more threatening feel to their writing.

Share some of the texts created in response to the photo and discuss how they have been successful in creating the specified moods.

Changing form

(k!) Planning activity: Writing for genres

Recap on knowledge about how drama scripts differ from prose before starting this section.

Students could be grouped into fours to read Text G, the extract from *An Inspector Calls*, so each person could have a part to read.

Activity 8 This activity uses *An Inspector Calls* by J.B. Priestley (Text G), and Worksheet 21h.

a Model how to change the form from script to prose. This could be quite short but focus on using first-person narrative and revealing personal feelings about the police calling. It may be appropriate to allow up to 15 minutes for students to plan and write a short response. Alternatively, write an opening line for each character on a board and show students how the text has been used to provide ideas about their character, for example, writing as Sheila: 'It was horrible when the Inspector explained how the girl had killed herself. I felt shocked.' Encourage less confident students to use the provided ideas as a starting point, whereas more able students may be able to create their own. Remind students of the need to select words according to what effect they wish to have on their audience. Again, following the prompts will provide a basic structure.

b Encourage students to share their texts and comment on each other's work. Focus peer attention on word choice and structure to ensure it is suitable for the task.

Developing ideas

The final activity is similar to the sort of task that may be presented in a controlled assessment. Students may find it useful to look back through the work done in the chapter before starting to write their response to the activity.

Activity 9

ki Connecting comments activity: Writing in genre

Worksheet 21i will support this activity.

Choosing from either science-fiction or thriller should enable students to focus their learning and create a text that shows aspects of their chosen genre. Encourage independent work on the writing task, though planning for writing could be shared if appropriate.

Students may share their texts either as a final version or a draft. Encourage peers to consider the success of the texts within the identified genre and to pick out aspects which let them know which genre had been chosen.

Stretch yourself

More able students may be able to develop their writing skills further by the challenge of using the same line but attempting to write in alternate genres. They should be encouraged to experiment with sentence structure, paragraphing and word choice in order to create different texts effectively.

Plenary

Check your learning Refer back to the aims of the chapter. Give students three minutes to list three

things they would expect to find in a specified genre of writing. Ask them to use one which they have studied during this chapter. Some students may need to look back through their notes and/or the Student Book to do this. Use discretion about to what extent they are permitted to do so as it may be more challenging to expect them to work from memory alone.

Make this more of a game by dividing the class into two teams. Each team has to challenge the other side to present features for a genre the opposing team names. For example, if Team A asks for 'Science-fiction', Team B has to present three features of that genre to score three points. If at any time the posing team (Team A in the example above) disagrees with what has been said they can challenge but have to explain to the satisfaction of the staff why the feature does not belong to that genre.

Outcomes

In this chapter your students have:

- learnt how to identify genres used in music, film and text
- learnt how to record features of different genres in text
- read a range of text extracts in different genres
- learnt how to identify features which contribute to the creation of genre in text
- experimented with writing in named genres
- peer assessed work and contributed to discussions about editing text
- utilised opportunities to practise for controlled assessments.

22 Making your writing skills count in the exam

AO focus

English AO3 Writing and English Language AO4 Writing

- Write [to communicate] clearly, effectively and imaginatively, using and adapting forms and selecting vocabulary appropriate to task and purpose in ways that engage the reader.

- Organise information and ideas into structured and sequenced sentences, paragraphs and whole texts, using a variety of linguistic and structural features to support cohesion and overall coherence.

- Use a range of sentence structures for clarity, purpose and effect, with accurate punctuation and spelling.

In this chapter your students will:

- learn about how their writing will be tested in the exam
- study questions in a sample paper
- plan, write and assess an answer
- read other students' answers and the examiner's comments on them.

Additional resources

Worksheets

22a: Questions for discussion
22b: Student responses to exam questions

Getting started

About the exam

In this short section students are provided with information about the structure and weighting of each section of the exam.

Provide students with the facts about the structure of the GCSE English and GCSE English Language exams using the information provided. Students need to be aware that the structure of the exam is quite fixed, so allocating specific time periods to each section is a beneficial thing to do as it ensures sufficient time for each part.

It may be useful for students who experience problems with recall, to look back through the Student Book at this point and identify which skills that will be used in the exam they have already revised, and to try and identify which ones they may need to revisit or work on again.

Ensure students understand that the writing tasks are intended to be of different lengths, so they should not be aiming to write the same amount for each response. Draw attention to the idea that planning and checking times are expected to be built in to what they write, so that editing skills are necessary to maximise chances of success.

Working through the chapter

How you can prepare for the exam

There is a quantity of information in this chapter that students need to be familiar with. The activities occur towards the end of the chapter, so it may be beneficial to break the section into smaller chunks to allow for 'absorption time', perhaps spread over a week.

In this section, students will have the chance to think about and discuss their feelings about exams. They are also provided with examples of ways that they can tackle their worries and fears pro-actively. This includes specific suggestions for ways of addressing the three main 'problem areas' for students.

Assessment Objectives

The AOs are broken down into more 'student friendly' words. Encourage discussion and asking of questions to ensure all students are clear about the various areas to be assessed. Refer to specific work students have done if they are uncertain or lack confidence in their ability to tackle any aspect.

What do these mean? How do they apply to each writing task?

Read through the information with students and ensure that the format of the questions and the expectations of the examiners are understood. Encourage students to ask questions about any areas that they do not understand. Check recall of terms like 'form', 'purpose', 'audience' and 'vocabulary'. It may be possible to incorporate the revision of these with some of the spelling techniques outlined above.

Alternatively, display the four words on a board or interactive whiteboard and give pairs of students sticky notes. Invite them to write their own explanation of two of the words onto the note and then place them with the words they have chosen. It should be possible to quickly go over the correct meanings and discuss any which have forgotten or misunderstood the terms. This will give a quick indication of how accurate their recall may be and may also show any areas of uncertainty about what each objective means.

The purpose of this whole chapter is to ensure students are familiar and confident about what will be expected of them in the exam. It is important to try and dispel the idea that it is not possible to revise for English exams and to enable students to see they can improve the chances of achieving the grade they desire by focusing on what the questions are asking and preparing to answer that.

It may be useful and reassuring to spend a few minutes at the beginning of the lesson to encourage the students to share some of their feelings and fears about exams generally, and English exams in particular. This could be done by grouping students into fours or sixes and providing each group with an A3 sheet of paper for them to wordstorm their responses. Alternatively, display A3 sheets around the room with questions written on and as students arrive invite them to record their opinions and ideas. These sheets could then be used as a focus for discussion.

Worksheet 22a has a range of suggested questions that could be used for either activity. The sheet can be customised to provide group or individual focus.

These are three areas which often cause difficulties for students in the Writing exam (spelling, sentences, paragraphs and planning). You may wish to provide some additional support for these areas.

The three areas indicated (Spelling, Structure and Planning) are the most common issues raised by students about English exams. It may be appropriate to consider grouping students depending upon their perceived difficulty with these areas and encouraging each group to undertake some peer assessed work. Focus attention on the Top Tips sections to answer some of the concerns/queries that students may raise.

Alternatively, you may wish to carry out some explicit teaching in areas in which students feel they need further work. The suggestions which follow are only some ways that these topics could be addressed. These could be taught to small groups as organised in the three main areas or provided to individual students for whom this sort of activity will offer some reassurance.

Spelling

Identify up to ten words which you know students find hard to spell. Then, try out some of these different ways to help to learn them:

1   Use the 'Look, Say, Cover, Write, Check' method. This involves:

- **Look** really hard at each word, one at a time.
- **Say** the word aloud – try saying a letter at a time or a syllable at a time.
- **Cover** the word over and then use their memory to write it down.
- **Check** what they have written against the correct version.

This activity could be done in pairs with students helping each other to learn tricky spellings.

2   Get a friend or family member to help students to learn them. Spell each word out taking it in turns to add a letter each. One person should start with the first letter, the other follows with the second etc. Again, this could be done in pairs, or for longer words that puzzle the whole group a larger number of students could be involved. Provide visual reinforcement of the spelling by having someone else write in on a board or interactive whiteboard as each letter is given.

3   Use mnemonics to create individualised ways of recalling spellings. Tell students to write the words down vertically instead of horizontally. Then suggest they choose a word to go with each letter to make a sentence. They should then try to visualise and/or draw the image created by the sentence. Give the example of the common and well-known sentence 'Big elephants can't always use small entrances' to recall the spelling of 'because'. Invite students to share their ideas, though often the most successful mnemonics are those which are completely personal to the student who is trying to remember it.

4   Suggest students use a list of spellings to copy the words. Encourage them to do this on different surfaces without actually using a pen! They should use their pointing finger and 'write' the word on table tops, work surfaces, carpets, walls ... anything that has a slightly different 'feel' to it. This tactile way of practising assists the neural pathways to be established to help with physical recall of spellings.

Sentences and paragraphs

Use Chapters 13 and 15–17 in this book to help students revise their skills in writing in sentences and paragraphs. These cover the basic matter of punctuation as well as different sentences structures, why to start new paragraphs and how to vary vocabulary. It may be useful to recap on the skills in these areas by revisiting some of the tasks set in the chapters.

If work carried out on those chapters is still available on displays or in books, put students into small groups and challenge them to condense the main points into a format that would be suitable to use as a revision mat. Each group should present their ideas and vote for the best one. These could then be shared between the students.

Use a quick starter activity to revise types of sentences. Ask students to write five sentences about something straightforward, for example, what they watch on TV/their favourite food but to use examples of all three sentence structures that they learnt about in Chapter 17 Working in pairs, each student should exchange their work with another and check that each one has included simple, compound and complex sentences.

Planning for an exam answer

Remind students about the work done previously on planning and that a plan of answers could help them write better answers. Ask students to explain what aspects of planning are important. Answers could include: a plan may give a structure to work round and reminds you of the ideas you had about what to include in your answer; plans should be brief, but useful; a long draft should be avoided as the exam does not allow enough time for this. Plans might take the form of one of the following methods:

- A list of topics you wish to include in your response.
- A mind map with linked points.
- A spidergram with sequenced ideas.
- A linear plan with ideas about which order points should be written in.

Invite students in groups to prepare examples of plans that they have used previously and share ideas about how/why each one is useful for different purposes.

The online resources may also help with addressing some of the issues raised by students linked with preparation for the exam.

Sample questions

Planning activity: Organising your ideas

Each question is broken down to provide pointers about the different parts of each question and

highlight what is expected to successfully address these elements.

Shorter writing task: Direct the students to work in pairs to review the task and outline, before working to produce a plan using the information provided about how to tackle this style of question. Share ideas about suitable planning methods and compare the different amounts of information that have been suggested for inclusion. It may be useful to discuss the issue of using personal details and what type of created persona could be reasonably substituted for that. Reassure students that this is acceptable as the exam is testing their ability to write in response to a set task – it is not assessing their truthfulness!

Students may already have relevant knowledge of writing a similar letter for their own work experience. Invite them to draw on this as it will provide a reminder that tasks in the exam may be linked with 'real life' expectations. However, the task itself still needs to be addressed. Students should not have the impression that they are able to disregard the question and adapt it to reflect their own knowledge.

Activity 1 In this activity students identify the purpose and audience for exam questions and the correct form for the response.

Longer writing task: it may be appropriate to encourage students to work on this task in a similar way to the shorter task above. Alternatively, group students according to their opinions about the question and ask small groups to prepare their points supporting that view. These can then be compared with the opposite side through discussion.

Check students understand that a range of question types could be set in this section – not all of which will necessarily involve explanation. Other opening instructions could include: Describe; Discuss; Inform or combinations of these. It may be helpful to explore with students that they understand the differences between each instruction.

More able students may prefer to try out the task independently. Encourage students to do the following to gain higher marks:

- Use bullet points to create a structure.
- Use paragraphs.

It may be useful to recap on the use of connectives for improving overall coherence, stressing that variety is important so avoid using a single ideas, for example, the repeated use of 'then' or 'first', 'second', etc.

Sample answers

🔲 On your marks activity: Analysing a Writing answer

The student responses to the tasks are included in the Student Book with examiner's comments. However, they are also available on Worksheet 22b without the examiner's comments. Students could be encouraged to go over the responses with the marking criteria in mind and identify how well they think each student has addressed the criteria. The examiner comments can be used to show how closely each response meets expectations and will help students identify areas for improvement.

There are opportunities for students to address the outlined task, or a very similar one, in order to build confidence in their writing abilities in this exam. It may assist students who have been granted Access Arrangements by AQA to utilise these in any practice work being done as this will help them understand the nature of their particular arrangements and learn how to work with staff who may be supporting them as a reader or scribe.

Shorter writing task

Students may find it useful to attempt one of the two activities independently, perhaps under exam conditions, as it will provide a more realistic context for their writing. Remind students that the actual time they should allow for this is about 20 minutes. If appropriate, after completing the writing, students could peer assess each other's work using the criteria and acting as an 'examiner'. Encourage students to provide feedback on the ways that the task has been successfully addressed and to identify two or three things that could be improved, perhaps using the examiner's response as a model. Their responses to the bulleted questions may assist in helping to identify any areas about which students are still unclear.

Activity 2 This is perhaps a slightly easier option as there is a model response already provided. It may be appropriate to direct students who lack confidence in their abilities to attempt this task and refer them to the example to give them a starting point. They should understand they need to consider how to make their own letter better than the one shown. Encourage students to use suitable examples as reasons why they should be considered for the placement. They should also be encouraged to draw on the plan they wrote during the earlier part of the chapter.

Activity 3 More confident students may be encouraged to try out this activity as a way of checking their skills and evaluating their abilities.

The response can be structured in a similar way to the first option, but it requires students to make specific choices about place of work and also think about how they present themselves as suitable employees. It might be helpful to remind students that they can make up relevant personal experience in order to make the response more interesting. Encourage students who tackle this task to stick to the time limit of 20 minutes and to still bear in mind the examiner's comments about the example. Students who are less confident may benefit from support to plan suitable points to include.

Longer writing task

It may also be suitable to use these practice questions as exam 'rehearsals'. The time allotted to this response should be about 40 minutes, including planning. Again, peer assessment of the completed responses could be beneficial in helping to secure understanding about marking criteria. Encourage students to think about the questions raised in the bulleted points – especially what advice could be given to improve the response.

The bullet points in the actual tasks should be used to provide a basic structure. Students who still find paragraphing an issue could be advised to at least start a new paragraph for each new bullet point they address. This will not be sufficient for real exam purposes, but may encourage them to be more confident about starting new paragraphs and reinforce work done previously on this topic.

It may be useful to remind students that they are not being asked to give a balanced, discursive view but one based on a single sided opinion with anecdotes and examples which support that perspective.

Activity 4

a Response is written from a pro-dog owning outlook so it may be difficult for some students to continue it if they do not agree with the writer. They may be better directed to the alternate activity. If students wish to take the opposite viewpoint i.e. that they would not enjoy owning a dog, they would need to start the whole response afresh rather than using the sample answer provided.

This task provides students with a starting point for their ideas, but also encourages them to look at the text critically and make changes to improve the response, thereby improving their editing skills. The examiner comments should be explored, with attention being paid to the points about vocabulary and the need to expand ideas beyond a single sentence. Support could be directed to assist students in planning which points to include in the subsequent parts of the question.

b The question invites students to put their views about sport from a pro- or anti-participant view. Encourage students to think in the widest terms about sport and not confine their comments to a single focus which they particularly like or dislike, for example, football. Refer to the examiner comments on the other task for this section to identify good practice in opening and continuing ideas – rhetorical questions and use of connectives to indicate continuing points. Remind students that in the longer writing task there will be a greater need for thinking about vocabulary as it is more likely the same words or phrases will appear, because of the single focus.

Plenary

Share responses to the tasks. It may be appropriate to allow for peer feedback and advice before feeding back to the whole class. Discuss whether responses meet the stated criteria for the exam tasks and link back any discussions to the earlier conversation about concerns in exams. It may be useful to revisit the question sheets and consider whether the work from this chapter has helped with preparation and to what extent students now feel they are able to revise exam skills. Concerns and worries discussed in the opening part of the chapter (Getting started) could be explicitly addressed. Students may be able to comment on how far they feel prepared for addressing exam-style questions. Remind students that continuing to revise their skills in those areas will be beneficial.

Outcomes

In this chapter your students have:

- improved accuracy of spelling
- understood ways to prepare for English/Language exams
- recapped on writing skills
- recapped on planning skills
- understood how to identify components of exam questions
- considered how to use forms appropriate to tasks
- participated in paired/group work on preparation to answer questions
- written responses to exam-style questions.

23 Making your writing skills count in the controlled assessment

AO focus

English AO3 Writing and English Language AO4 Writing

- Write [to communicate] clearly, effectively and imaginatively, using and adapting forms and selecting vocabulary appropriate to task and purpose in ways that engage the reader.

- Organise information and ideas into structured and sequenced sentences, paragraphs and whole texts, using a variety of linguistic and structural features to support cohesion and overall coherence.

- Use a range of sentence structures for clarity, purpose and effect, with accurate punctuation and spelling.

In this chapter your students will:

- learn more about how their writing is assessed in the controlled assessment

- learn more about the tasks in the controlled assessment and look at sample tasks

- read other students' answers and the teacher's comments on them.

Working through the chapter

What is controlled assessment?

The controlled assessment may be a new way of working for students so this chapter in the Student Book is intended to address questions and concerns they may have about this element of the qualification.

Students may need to have the precise arrangements for controlled assessments as they will be done at your centre explained to them. The way that the tasks are to be decided upon could also be explained at this point. Your centre may offer students the option to choose their own tasks, or may prescribe which ones to tackle depending on the teaching scheme agreed. It may also be useful to provide dates and times for the controlled assessment arrangements.

Explain that the exam board requirement is for students to write two pieces under controlled conditions. Spend some time with students exploring the key words linked with this type of assessment

so they are clear about each aspect of this. You may wish to use the following terms:

Controlled assessment terminology	
Controlled conditions	This is likely to be similar in nature to exam situations. Students will have to work independently, supervised by staff, probably in silence because discussion while producing the final written work is forbidden.
Guidance time allowance	This will be how long AQA has said students may spend writing their final written work. The work will have to be submitted at the end of that time.
Word limit	The approximate number of words AQA suggests is submitted to ensure the response is of enough length to show all the assessment objectives have been addressed.
Formal assessment period	The time spent on the response which will be supervised. This does not include any preparation or research time set as independent study or homework.
Tasks	This is the piece of work required by AQA as part of your GCSE course assessment.

Focus attention on whichever qualification is being addressed – GCSE English or GCSE English Language. Read through the requirements for each GCSE in terms of which task bank will be available and discuss the requirement for a certain word length. Students may need reassuring that counting every word to 'hit' the word total will not be necessary or useful. It may be helpful to individuals to work out the approximate number of lines/pages they would need to write to be close to the required total. This can be done quite easily by using material they have already written and averaging out how many words they have on each line of an A4 page (over ten lines perhaps) and working from that to see how many lines/pages that would equate to.

Students will need to understand the constraints of the controlled assessment and what they are not permitted to do. Draw attention to the bullet points which outline these.

Introducing the tasks

'Moving images' and 'Prompts and re-creations/ Re-creations' are common to both the GCSE English and the GCSE English Language qualifications.

The other tasks for each qualification are included in the bulleted lists. Draw attention to the main difference between exam and controlled assessment. It may be useful for students to discuss the implications of the expanded time frame and the known aspect of the question and text.

Remind students that the AOs for both exam and controlled assessment remain the same. Students benefit from knowing the precise areas that are being assessed so that writing can be targeted for specific skills.

Preparing for the controlled assessment

The record keeping aspect of the preparation time may be something else that students will be unfamiliar with and this may require further explanation. Your centre may have a pro forma that students will be required to use for recording sources. This would be an appropriate time to outline this and demonstrate how it will be used. Any other strategies individual to your centre may need to be addressed before moving on to consider the nature of the tasks to be done.

Sample tasks and answers

The following paragraphs outline the parameters and expectations of the different tasks that may be addressed by students. Draw attention to the ones relevant to the appropriate qualification being taken. Each section suggests ways to address that type of task and provides some of the key words that may be associated with the instructions.

Moving images (GCSE English and GCSE English Language)

- *kl* On your marks activity: 'Moving images' task
- *kl* Video case study activity: 'Moving images' video

Unlike the other tasks, this one will be based exclusively on material that is based on film, TV or video. Students will probably benefit from having read a number of different reviews in order to identify the way they are generally structured and be able to have a bank of models on which to draw for this. Web-based reviews may also be a useful resource for students to consider as part of the preparation for this task.

The e-resources contain some material which may assist students with understanding the different ways that a media response can be written.

Moving Images key words	
Review	These are written to comment on the quality of something to provide information to others who may wish to buy/watch/hear the thing being reviewed. They are often written when something new is launched for the first time and may appear in magazines, newspapers or on TV or radio shows.

Activity 1 This provides students with a chance to generate ideas based on their own choice of film. Encourage them to think carefully about their own choice of descriptive language, just as the director of a film would think carefully about lighting, sound effects and so on. Students could work in pairs or small groups to generate an interesting and varied range of vocabulary. They can begin to draft a section of a response for part c, which could then be compared with the example Text A on page 153.

Prompts and re-creations/Re-creations (GCSE English and GCSE English Language)

- *kl* Connecting comments activity: Changing texts for a 'Re-creations' task
- *kl* On your marks activity: 'Re-creations' task

These tasks may be based upon poems in the *AQA Anthology*. Encourage students to consider ways that alternate views of any situation can be gathered. For example, invite groups of students to consider how many people might be 'involved' in one way or another in a bank robbery. Their ideas may include bank staff, robbers, customers, security guards. Then invite students to consider how the same situation could be regarded in different ways depending on the viewpoint of each participant. It may be useful to allocate roles and ask each student (in role) in such a scene to express a couple of sentences which give an idea about their mood or feelings about the robbery. This is an exercise which allows students to have an understanding of how a situation might be used to show alternate views from the one given in a text. Lead from this into considering some of the key words linked with such tasks:

Re-creations key words	
Continue	Students will be expected to use the extract provided and move the ideas on with their own creative views. The extract could come from a range of sources and be in prose, drama or poetry.
Transform	Students will be provided with a piece of text as a focus. They will be asked to change the way the text is presented. This could be via altering the form, so changing from a poem to a script. In English Language, students may be asked to transform the text into a non-fiction piece or newspaper article.

For GCSE English you could offer your students the chance to develop an idea based on a prompt. A number of different prompts may be provided.

These could include: a single sentence of text; an image; a verse from a poem; a line from a song; a headline; a 'blurb'; a pen portrait. They will be able to choose the form in which they want to continue the ideas provided.

Students need to be aware that the scope for developing ideas can be wide. There is no 'correct' story or form that teachers will be seeking. The skills which will be most useful are based in imagination. Wide reading of a range of texts may encourage students to experiment with genres and character. The chapter which addresses this may be a useful source of ideas for revision of the skills that will be needed.

The poem provided, 'She Pops Home' by Cal Clothier (Text B), may not be one that students have studied previously. However, this will allow students the chance to read and consider ways to respond to this type of task.

Before reading the student response, you may wish to organise students into small groups and invite them to read through the poem text and work out what attitude the different characters in the poem each show. Direct them to pick out aspects of the text which show what the girl referred to as 'she' seems to be like (her personality and behaviour). They may also be able to comment on the girl's parents and how they feel about her visits. Ask them to create a scenario in which these events could take place. These could be shared with the rest of the group.

Move from this to consider the student's response in the Student Book and the teacher's comments which follow.

Activity 2

a Engaging with the transformation in role as the girl may students who need some support from the text. The references in the response to some phrases in the poem are praised, so this should be encouraged to link the creative writing firmly with the text. More able students may wish to rewrite the text entirely, which may help improve their confidence with this type of task.

b The scripting task is possibly the more difficult of the two as it uses a less familiar form. However, it may be appropriate to refer students to look again at the work in Chapter 19 which deals with script writing. The change of form from poem to script may offer students a chance to experiment before having to tackle a similar question in the actual controlled assessment.

Prompts key phrases	
Write a creative piece	This direction may be linked with an opening or final line of a text. Students will need to decide how they can best use that line to demonstrate their writing skills.

Me. Myself. I. (GCSE English)

This part of the controlled assessment will be based on personal experiences, beliefs and opinions. Students should expect that most of this writing may be autobiographical. They may be invited to write in a way that reflects something that has occurred in their own life or to give their opinion about an issue which has affected them. They will be invited to choose which form they feel is most suitable to reflect their ideas which should provide a wide scope for their writing. It may be useful to refer to chapters in the Writing section which support the planning of autobiography as part of the revision for this task. Students may already have a range of ideas which could be developed.

Try to be sensitive to individuals who may struggle with looking into their past or drawing on those experiences. Remind students that 'creative writing' should be exactly that, so they are free to use other people's experiences or anecdotes if their own are not something they wish to use.

Me. Myself. I. key phrases	
Personal Experience	This is the key phrase in all writing in this section. These words may not appear in each task, but the underlying expectation will be that students write in a way that shows their personal involvement with the topic. It will probably need to be written in first-person and reveal aspects of their feelings, thoughts and beliefs.
Choose a form	This instruction is intended to offer students the chance to decide how they want to present their ideas. The three main forms are: prose, drama and poetry. If students choose to use poetry, it will be necessary for them to write more than one poem and possibly also a commentary.

The short opening section of the student answer (Text D) is intended to stimulate ideas rather than provide a full exemplar response. Focus student attention on the teacher's comments and the things which have been done well, for example, vocabulary variety, sentence variety and focus on the task.

a Recap on the ways that planning can be done, then ask students to create their own plan before starting the writing itself. The focus of the question is on 'impact on your life' so it might be useful to emphasise this point as students will need to ensure that they demonstrate this throughout their writing on this question.

b They should only aim to write the opening paragraph, but use similar positive aspects as the example in the Student Book. Some students may benefit from support with sentence variety. Invite students to share their openings with another student and comment on how interesting/ effective they find these to be. Encourage each student to check the other's work for the positive aspects outlined by the teacher.

Stretch yourself

Some students may profit from being able to expand their initial paragraph into a longer piece. This could perhaps be suitable as a homework task as this will also encourage independence. Encourage students to use the plan they devised and think about how each section could be linked to the next through word choices, as in the example.

Commissions (GCSE English Language)

On yours marks activity: 'Commissions' task

This task allows students to express their opinions in an unrestricted way, except for the constraints of the form of writing. These may be linked with writing for a particular media. Students may need reminding that a word limit imposed for this task will need to be strictly observed. The tasks are likely to be non-fiction writing. It is important that students remember to maintain their focus on the purpose and audience specified.

Commissions key terms	
Write a piece	Students will be expected to write in a style that has already been suggested in the task. It is likely that this will be a non-fiction task. It is probable that the task will suggest the response should be prose and based on their own views or opinions.

Discuss with students what they understand by the term 'Passions'. Comments may be serious or humorous. Ensure that students understand that both are acceptable as written forms for the controlled assessment, though both need to be carefully planned.

Focus attention on the AOs that are being addressed and working in pairs, ask students to read through the response and identify if and where they have been met.

Their next task is to offer advice about improving what has been written. Students are being asked to behave as teachers and consider the writing in a similar way to the examples seen earlier in the chapter. The feedback from this exercise may be done as a whole group discussion in order to maximise the number of ideas offered and provide a wide audience for the points.

Activity 4

a The first option asks students to identify a topic about which they want to write. Encourage students to pick something about which they have an opinion even if they do not regard it as a 'Passion'. Support may be offered to assist students with developing their ideas and using anecdotes to back up their views. Invite students to share their writing with a small group and take responses and questions about it.

b The topic suggested in the second option is an open subject. Students need to consider what the most appropriate form and content may be for their audience. The writing also must appeal to the reader through careful choice of vocabulary. This may be a challenging task as it is important that students do not regard it as simply an opportunity to rant about something they dislike, or to move between a range of subjects which annoys them. Support for planning before starting the task may be useful and improve the focus on 'Pet Hates'. Encourage students to think about a single topic and develop a series of points about it which can be linked through language use.

Plenary

Check your learning Check that students are equipped with the information they feel they need in order to be confident about tackling controlled assessments. Ask individuals to feed back what has been learnt about these assessments. Suggest that in pairs students devise three pieces of advice that should be remembered when tackling these questions and encourage these to be shared between pairs. Each pair should then agree on three joint pieces of advice before explaining these to the remainder of the class.

Refer back to the starter activity when students learnt the meanings of some of the specific vocabulary connected with controlled assessment. Challenge students to define the same terms now in their own words to demonstrate that they have understood the vocabulary they need. It may be useful for these ideas to be recorded to provide a range of ways for students to understand the words.

Outcomes

In this chapter your students have:

- understood the nature of controlled assessments
- learnt about the Assessment Objectives that they need to address
- learnt to tackle differing styles of tasks in different ways
- identified ways to improve their writing in order to be more successful
- addressed a range of questions based on the AQA exemplar.

Section C: Speaking and listening

Overview

Section C of the Student Book is designed to develop students' skills in reading as defined by the Assessment Objectives for GCSE English (AO1 Speaking and listening) and GCSE English Language (AO1 Speaking and listening) and tested in the controlled assessments.

GCSE English: AO1 Speaking and listening

GCSE English Language: AO1 Speaking and listening

- Speak to communicate clearly and purposefully; structure and sustain talk, adapting it to different situations and audiences; use Standard English and a variety of techniques as appropriate.
- Listen and respond to speakers' ideas and perspectives, and how they construct and express meanings.
- Interact with others, shaping meanings through suggestions, comments and questions and drawing ideas together.
- Create and sustain different roles.

The chapters provide opportunities for students to draw on and revise the skills they have already acquired in speaking and listening, and to develop these further. The learning objectives, founded in the assessment objectives but in 'student-friendly' language, are given at the start of each chapter. Throughout each chapter the learning points are clarified and modelled, and followed by activities which are designed to reinforce and extend students' learning.

Students are encouraged to work independently or in pairs or small groups, as appropriate, and are given regular opportunities to assess their personal progress and that of other students, often against fixed criteria. The learning within the units is cumulative, building on what has come before, and at the end of several chapters there is a summative activity which challenges students to demonstrate their learning across the whole section.

Each chapter can be used as a discrete stand-alone topic with activities and tasks specific to the named objectives. They do not have to be done in the order in which they appear in the Student Book, though it is worth noting that this order was arrived at after careful consideration of how best to build students' skills in speaking and listening.

Assessment

GCSE English and GCSE English Language
Controlled assessment: Three equally weighted activities.

- Presenting
- Discussing and listening
- Role playing.

Nelson Thornes resources

Chapter	Student Book activities	kerboodle! resources
24 Your speaking and listening skills	1: Paired discussion as to what makes a good speaker using images for stimulus 2: Prioritising good speaking skills to form 'Top 5 Tips' 3: Preparing a short talk; using the 'Top 5 Tips' to peer assess a partner's talk 4: Prioritising good listening skills to form 'Top 5 Tips' 5: Preparing a short talk; listening to a partner's talk using 'Top 5 Tips' for listening 6–7: Analysing and practising using body language 8: Self-evaluation quiz of speaking and listening skills 9: Paired discussion offering advice to students who want to improve their speaking and listening skills Check your learning: Recapping good speaking and listening skills	• Worksheet 24a: Effective speakers • Worksheet 24b: Good listeners • Worksheet 24c: Evaluating and improving your speaking and listening skills • Learning activity: Speaking and listening terms • Audio case study activity: Effective speakers • Video case study activity: Good listeners • Analysis activity: Understanding body language
25 Presentation	1: Identifying when you might be required to make a presentation 2: Understanding more about how GCSE presentations will be assessed 3: Making notes on the structure of a presentation 4: Selecting appropriate vocabulary to use in a presentation 5: Deciding when it would be appropriate to use Standard English in a presentation 6: Anticipating questions and answers as part of a presentation 7: Using the planning guidance to plan and deliver a presentation; assessing your presentation Check your learning: Recapping understanding of key terms linked to presentations	• Worksheet 25a: Giving a talk • Audio role-play activity: Presenting your view • Audio role-play activity: Giving a talk • Learning activity: Using Standard English • Learning activity: Top presentation tips
26 Discussing and listening	1: Understanding different ways to make a positive contribution to a discussion 2–3: Practising asking questions to help the speaker develop their points 4: Planning contributions to a discussion 5: Practice group discussion based around encouraging local people to use a shopping centre Review and reflect: Assessing performance in the group discussion task Check your learning: Recapping the features of good group work	• Worksheet 26a: Putting it together • Learning activity: Positive group work • Video case study activity: An interview • Learning activity: Group work roles • Analysis activity: Group behaviour
27 Role play	1: Experimenting with using facial expressions and gestures to create character 2: Reflecting on how you have interacted with others in different situations 3: Suggesting a range of characteristics for a character; preparing a character plan 4: Role-play practice 1 Review and reflect: Self-assessment of the role play 5: Role-play practice 2: Preparing the character plan Review and reflect: Self-assessment and target setting 6: Practising and delivering the role play Check your learning: Recapping key terms linked to role play	• Worksheet 27a: Playing a character • Analysis activity: Characters of the imagination • Analysis activity: Finding characters • Audio role-play activity: Hot-seating a character

Chapter	Student Book activities	kerboodle! resources
28 Making your Speaking and listening skills count in the controlled assessment	1–3: Reviewing key terms linked to speaking and listening tasks 4: Using teacher summaries of example tasks to decide which performance is stronger and why Check your learning: Recapping understanding the Speaking and listening controlled assessments	• Connecting comments activity: Effective group work • Planning activity: Planning a presentation • On your marks activity: Role play

Student checklist worksheet

Use the questions below to assess your Speaking and listening skills and to set your personal Speaking and listening targets.

Skill	Very confident	Quite confident	Sometimes I can	Often I can't	Which chapters might help?
Speak clearly to communicate my ideas					24
Use Standard English when appropriate					25
Structure my presentations effectively					25
Listen to the other views					26
Ask questions					26
Make suggestions and comments					26
Draw ideas together					26
Take on and sustain different roles					27
Use voice, vocabulary and gesture to create a role					27

Use your responses to the checklist to set yourself *no more than* three targets to achieve from the Speaking and listening section.

1...

2...

3...

Checking students' progress

The tasks below are all included in the Student Book and can be used to check student progress in a particular skill.

Chapters	A focus	Suggested strategies.
25	• Speak to communicate clearly and purposefully; structure and sustain talk; use Standard English and a variety of techniques as appropriate	**Chapter 25, Activity 8** **Students:** • give a 5-minute presentation aimed at a group of Year 9 students • organise and structure their presentation logically and clearly • use a range of vocabulary relevant to their audience • use Standard English when appropriate • answer questions effectively and using relevant detail.
26	• Listen and respond to speaker's ideas, perspectives and how they construct and express their meanings • Interact with others, shaping meanings through suggestions, comments and questions and drawing together	**Chapter 26, Activity 5** **Students:** • contribute to a group discussion, taking an active role • speak and explain their ideas clearly • use Standard English when appropriate • listen to others' ideas and ask relevant questions • use appropriate body language and gestures.
27	• Create and sustain different roles	**Chapter 27, Activities 4–5** **Students:** • prepare and deliver a role play based on a given scenario • work with a partner to plan the development of the role play • use tone of voice and body language to develop and sustain their character throughout the role play • speak clearly throughout.

General resources

The resources in the Student Book, Teacher's Book and *kerboodle!* provide a range of learning opportunities for students and give them practice at developing their skills using a wide variety of text types. The resources suggested below can be used to reinforce, develop and extend students' skills and learning further.

Context	Resources
Presenting The resources listed provide models of presentations, including speeches, to use as models of structure and language use.	• The Joint Exam Board DVD 2009 • Oration at the funeral of Princess Diana: Earl Spencer • 'I Have a Dream' speech by Martin Luther King • *Dragon's Den*: BBC Television • *The Apprentice*: BBC Television
Discussing The resources listed are useful in stimulating discussion in pairs or groups.	Celebrity: • *Jade was perfect victim*: Michael Parkinson The important things in life: • Song: 'Richard Corey' by Simon and Garfunkel War: • Song: 'Your King and Country Want You' • Poem: *Conquerors*: Henry Treece
Role playing These resources provide interesting stimulus materials for role play activities.	Poems: • *But You Didn't* by Merrill Glass (Bereavement) • *My Parents Kept Me* by Stephen Spender (Bullying) Short stories: • *The Oakum Room* by Theresa Tomlinson (Suppression / Breaking Free) • *Flight* by Doris Lessing (Growing Up) Songs: • 'Fixing to Die Rag' by Country Joe McDonald and The Fish (War) • 'She's Leaving Home' by The Beatles (Running away)

AO focus

English and English Language AO1 Speaking and listening

- Speak [to communicate] clearly and purposefully; structure and sustain talk, adapting it to different situations and audiences; use Standard English and a variety of techniques as appropriate.

- Listen and respond to speakers' ideas and perspectives and how they construct and express their meanings.

- Interact with others, shaping meanings through suggestions, comments and questions and drawing ideas together.

In this chapter your students will learn about:

- good speaking skills
- good listening skills
- the use of body language.

Additional resources

Worksheets

24a: Effective speakers

24b: Good listeners

24c: Evaluating and improving your speaking and listening skills

Getting started

🔘 Learning activity: Speaking and listening terms

The aim of this unit is to build on the skills and knowledge about speaking and listening that students have acquired throughout Key Stage 3.

It is likely that your students will cover a range of abilities in speaking and listening and that considerable skill will have to be exercised in ensuring that they all perform to their potential. Some may be confident speakers in a range of situations whereas others may not, some may have difficulty participating in active group work whereas others may not and some students may be uncomfortable with role play and as a result may exhibit inappropriate behaviour.

The activities in this unit will enable students to develop the qualities needed in speakers and listeners at Key Stage 4. These are designed to encourage students to work with increasing independence and to reflect on their own performances and those of others.

You could begin the teaching on this unit by asking students to work with a partner to reflect on Speaking and listening activities they have enjoyed at Key Stage 3. These could include activities where they have observed other students. The purpose of this is to remind students of the role that speaking and listening has to play in English lessons. You may wish to ask them to group their activities under the headings of making presentations, discussing and listening and creating and sustaining roles as preparation for work in the following chapters.

Activity 1 The aim of the picture activity is to raise students' awareness of effective speaking and listening skills drawing on their own experience.

b This part of the activity encourages students to think closely about the features of good listeners and speakers. Students could be asked to make notes on their ideas to share with the whole class. Students are likely to come up with some of the points listed in Activity 2 but their own interpretation of good speaking and listening skills should be respected.

Working through the chapter

What makes a good speaker?

🔘 Audio case study activity: Effective speakers

Activity 2

a The first part of the activity presents students with a list of characteristics of good speakers. Before starting the activity you may find it useful to discuss the statements with students to ensure that they have a clear understanding of these. A good outcome of this discussion would be for the students to come up with examples to exemplify each statement.

b Other characteristics students may suggest might include:

- taking turns
- asking when they do not understand
- adding to points that have been made
- introducing new ideas to discussions
- maintaining eye contact with the audience.

c   Once students have added their own ideas to this list, they can work with a partner to prepare their Top 5 Tips for speaking. They will use these in Activity 3 as the basis for their evaluation. If appropriate, you could ask each pair to share their top tips with the rest of the class and then have a vote on what students think are the most important. The final Top 5 Tips could be displayed on a class Speaking and listening notice board.

Activity 3 This activity provides the students with an opportunity to rehearse and peer assess a short performance using the criteria agreed in Activity 2 as a basis for evaluation. You will need to allow students time for planning their talks either in class or as a homework activity. Some may need encouragement to think of reasons to explain why they enjoyed the activity they have chosen.

Peer assessment and peer encouragement have an important part to play in Speaking and listening activities. Before feedback is given you may wish to take time to talk with students about how to give feedback.

The following points could be raised:

- Feedback is intended to be a positive experience.
- It is useful to begin by drawing on the positive features of a performance.
- Areas for improvement should be clearly signalled by reference to agreed criteria.

Review and reflect

Part of the preparation for the controlled assessment tasks in the Speaking and listening unit could be the production of a speaking and listening portfolio where students record their targets and reflections after a range of tasks. The first entry could be their reflections on feedback from their talk in Activity 3. They could also file their Top 5 Tips in the portfolio.

What makes a good listener?

Video case study activity: Good listeners

You will already be aware of the wide range of listening skills within your classes and of the link between good listening skills and high levels of concentration. It is important that students are encouraged to see the importance of good listening skills in their lives as a whole and not just in their English lessons.

Before starting Activity 4 you may wish to revise/re-introduce listening skills to the whole class by playing a recording of news items and asking students to identify the main points. Another

simple starter could be to ask students to pause for 60 seconds and make a note of all of the sounds they can hear around them.

Activity 4
The list of characteristics of good listeners in the Student Book could be expanded with some of the following:

- are open to new ideas
- are able to comment on what has been said
- sometimes add to or refine what has been said
- ask helpful questions.

As in Activity 2, pairs can share their Top Tips with the rest of the class and agree the criteria for what good listeners do. They could be displayed on a notice board or recorded in the student speaking and listening portfolio.

Activity 5 Students can now work in pairs to rehearse and peer assess a short performance using the criteria agreed in Activity 4 as a basis for evaluation. As before, allow students time to plan their talk, remind them that the focus here is on their listening skills.

In Chapter 26 there is a section which provides a detailed focus on the use of closed and open questions. However, before beginning Activity 5 you may wish to discuss the skill of how to ask good questions with students, giving them examples of both closed and open questions and asking them to decide which are more helpful to a speaker. This should ensure that the listening partner is able to carry out the task more confidently.

Examples of closed questions:

- How often do you watch your favourite TV show?
- Who is your least favourite character?

Examples of open questions:

- Can you explain what you like most about your favourite character?
- Can you tell me why you like horror films so much?

Students could also be coached in how to ask supplementary questions to help their partner extend their ideas. For example: Can you describe a memorable scene in which your favourite character appeared?

Review and reflect

As before, feedback comments and targets for improvement could be recorded in the speaking and listening portfolio.

Body language

(kl) Analysis activity: Understanding body language

You could introduce the activity by miming a series of different moods for the students and asking them to guess the feelings being portrayed.

Activity 6 This activity provides a picture stimulus for non-verbal communication. You could ask students to identify the gestures they think are positive and which are negative. Once students have had an opportunity to 'interpret' the sample gestures, they might share their ideas with a partner or the rest of the class.

Activity 7 This activity gives students a chance to practise using gestures and body language as they speak. The task suggests a new, short talk to a partner but if you prefer, students could revisit one of the talks they prepared for Activities 2 or 4 and add gestures to this.

Evaluating your skills

Activity 8 The quiz is also included on Worksheet 24c, which can be handed out to students.

The questions in the quiz are based on the Speaking and listening criteria in the AQA specification. They can be used as an introduction to the range of skills that students are expected to demonstrate at Key Stage 4. Their purpose is to enable students to give an honest assessment of their current abilities and to give them a clear idea of targets for improvement.

Before they tackle the quiz it may be helpful to students to give them an explanation of some of the terms they may not understand, for example:

- complex ideas
- appropriate vocabulary
- sentence structures.

Once students have completed the charts with their scores they should be encouraged to comment on the feedback with a partner. Comments could include whether each student has given an accurate assessment of their own abilities (some students regularly underestimate themselves) and if not, what changes need to be made.

You may wish to ask the students to complete the quiz again after a period of a few months to see if their scores have changed and to reflect on the areas where they have made improvements.

How can I improve my speaking and listening?

Although the problem page letters appear to be light-hearted, they cover a range of difficulties commonly encountered by students. They also provide a model for students to analyse their own difficulties and weaknesses. The reading of the letters and the subsequent discussion will provide a useful opportunity for practising small group discussion.

Activity 9 In discussing the problems and in finding solutions students should develop an awareness of how to improve their own speaking and listening skills. It could be useful to ask them which of the problems they identify with.

Producing written replies to the letters could be set as a homework task or a task for independent writing.

Plenary

Check your learning Now that your students have worked through the chapter you could ask them to set their individual targets in speaking and listening. Students should be encouraged to look back at their scores in Activity 5 to help them set their targets. Some may need guidance in setting realistic targets. For example, if a student has difficulty in creating a memorable character in role plays (5–7) there is little point in them selecting a role play comment from the highest level of achievement (14–15). They should select their target from the next range above, for example, use language and gesture to create characters.

Their responses in this section should be recorded in their speaking and listening portfolio so that they can refer to and review their targets on a regular basis.

Outcomes

In this chapter your students have:

- thought carefully about the skills needed by good speakers and listeners
- practised their listening skills
- reflected on the role of body language and gesture in speaking and listening
- identified their strengths as a speaker and listener
- reflected on ways to improve their own speaking and listening skills
- peer assessed others to help improve skills.

25 Presentation

AO focus

English and English Language AO1 Speaking and listening

- Speak [to communicate] clearly and purposefully; structure and sustain talk, adapting it to different situations and audiences; use Standard English and a variety of techniques as appropriate.

In this chapter your students will learn about:

- the key features which help to make a 'good' presentation
- how to plan, prepare and deliver a presentation.

Additional resources

Worksheets

25a: Giving a talk

Getting started

An appropriate starter activity could be to ask students to write anonymously on post-it notes some of the negative and positive points about giving presentations. The students could place their notes on a notice board or you could select some of the notes to lead a plenary activity discussing issues that have been raised. The purpose of this would be to make students aware that often their own misgivings are shared by other students.

Working through the chapter

The aim of this lesson is to enable students to understand the key features involved in planning and delivering a presentation to a group of their peers and/or adults. For many students this is a very daunting task and they will need constant reassurance as they complete the activities.

Activity 1 The aim of this activity is help students focus on the range of situations both in and out of school when presentational skills are required. It is intended to enable them to understand the importance of developing these skills.

Other occasions when a presentation is required could include:

- Making a speech in a school council meeting.
- Giving a vote of thanks or making a speech to welcome a visitor to school.
- A witness account in court.
- A job interview.

What makes a good presentation?

This section is intended to raise awareness and consolidate understanding of the key features which underpin good presentations.

You may wish to go through the bullet points with students and ask them about their understanding of each of the bullet points.

Suggested responses are:

- Organisation: the order of the content and how it is arranged.
- Vocabulary: the range, choice and appropriateness of words used.
- Standard English: the forms of words, grammar and sentence structures which would be recognised and understood in any part of the UK, it is generally used in formal situations.
- Response: the way in which points are raised and questions which are asked, are then dealt with.

Organisation

Activity 2 Alerting students to the presentation they will be working on and delivering later in the chapter will give them plenty of time for reflection. Thinking of three suitable topics from which they make a final choice could make a brief homework task.

Some students may find the selection of a topic rather daunting. It may be useful to make clear from the outset that students can approach you for help with the choice of topic.

A useful activity at this point could be one which asks student to focus on the advantages and disadvantages of using the listed methods of presentation.

- PowerPoint: many students find using this makes them feel very secure; however, too many detailed slides can lead to them reading aloud rather than presenting. PowerPoint works well if used to support a presentation perhaps with a series of images or a set of facts to lend emphasis.

- Visual stimuli: these can be projected on to a whiteboard and can lend a very striking focus to a talk. The pitfalls of these are that some students turn their back on their audience and talk to the images. Passing photographs round the class during a talk can lead to distraction among the audience; these are better displayed on a board at the front.

- Note cards: these are essential for all but the most accomplished of speakers, but if the notes are too detailed or there are too many cards then students over-rely on them and can end up reading from them instead of talking to their audience.

Activity 3 You could emphasise to students that they must choose a topic in which they are interested. Sometimes students choose a topic at random and their lack of engagement can become apparent in the delivery of their presentation.

a Students may wish to discuss their short list of topics with partner.

b Deciding on key points is an essential part of planning, some students may need assistance from a partner or teaching assistant in ensuring that they have enough key points to make a detailed and interesting presentation. Five key points if well developed should be sufficient.

c Students should be encouraged to think carefully about the order and which point will have the most impact on their audience. Is it the one they will put first? Will they save one point to make an interesting or dramatic ending?

d You may wish to check the timings students put on their plan as sometimes they make unrealistic judgements about how long a particular point will take to deliver – for many students finishing too soon is a common mistake.

Vocabulary

You could begin this section by asking students to think of three reasons why vocabulary is such an important feature of a successful presentation. Some likely reasons are as follows:

- If you use too many long words for a student audience they may lose interest and switch off.

- If your words are all the same your audience will get bored.

- It is the vocabulary that makes a talk interesting – your words can entertain, surprise an audience, etc.

Activity 4

a A thesaurus may help students to select their descriptive words.

b This may not be necessary for students who are talking about a topic such as their family.

c Thinking about vocabulary beforehand is essential to the success of the presentation. Once students have noted down their vocabulary they may wish to share their ideas with another student for comment and suggestions for additions.

d Students could use a thesaurus taking the words on the list as a starting point.

Using a range of language

This section not only focuses students on the importance of making their presentation interesting and engaging by the use of a range of language, it also puts focus on how to use language effectively in their introduction to grab their audience's attention.

An alternative approach to the use of the sample texts could be to display Text A and Text B on a whiteboard and ask the students to decide which text is most likely to grab the interest of listeners. Following that you could annotate both texts following students' suggestions to highlight the good points of Text B and the weak points of Text A.

You could then ask them to look at the annotations in the Student Book to see how close their suggestions were.

🔊 Audio role-play activity: Presenting your view

🔊 Video case study activity: Giving a talk

Activity 5 Writing the introduction to their presentation and trying it out on a partner will be the first chance for students to see if their presentation is likely to be successful. As they are only asked to write a very small amount here it will not be too difficult for them to broaden their range of vocabulary if necessary. This short task will also give you the chance to observe those students who may struggle with this task and provide them with additional support.

As a plenary to this part of the lesson you may wish to ask more confident students to present their introductions to the whole class for feedback. In this way good practice will be modelled for the rest of the class whether it is by using vocabulary to engage the audience in the introduction or by making adjustments following constructive feedback.

Standard English

🔊 Learning activity: Using Standard English

Before using the definitions in the Student Book you may wish to ask students to give their own definitions of Standard English.

Activity 6 When making their choices students should be encouraged to justify their decisions either to a partner or to the whole class. Likely responses and reasons for choice are in the following table.

Likely response and reasons for choice	
a	Standard English as a head teacher talking to parents in a presentation is a formal situation.
b	Presentation of a new product in a shopping centre is likely to be a mixture of Standard English for a formal situation and non-Standard English some of the time to appeal more directly to an audience of shoppers.
c	Year 11 students making a presentation in an assembly would use Standard English as this is a formal situation and a formal topic, e.g. a charity appeal. However, there could also be occasional use of non-Standard English to get their audience (younger students) on their side.
d	Year 11 students talking to parents would use Standard English for a formal situation and also as a sign of respect.
e	Standard English only is the norm in job presentations.
f	A politician would use Standard English in a formal situation and to get his/her message across to a wide range of people across the UK.
g	This would include some Standard English for a formal presentation but also non-Standard English as they are talking to their own peer group.

Response

It should be stressed to students that good planning for a successful presentation extends to planning for potential questions.

Activity 7 After writing down possible questions and answers it may be helpful to students to share these with a partner who may be able to think of additional questions.

With this, as with other aspects of preparing for a presentation, students can gain in confidence if they have rehearsed at appropriate intervals and have received feedback from a peer.

This could perhaps be a suitable point to revise with students the work done on open and closed questions in Chapter 24. Students in the group could be reminded of the usefulness in asking open questions to assist fellow students to extend their ideas and improve the quality of their presentation.

Making your presentation

(k!) Learning activity: Top presentation tips
Rehearsal time should be given to students to ensure that they do their best. This could perhaps be a homework task. For many students considerable rehearsal time is needed to ensure that they are confident enough to deliver without looking too often at notes or even reading from them.

Presentations could be delivered throughout a whole lesson, although sometimes the attention of the audience can wane if they have to listen to too many talks. After every presentation the audience should be encouraged to ask questions of the presenter. Using the start of lessons to listen to a few presentations over a period of a few weeks can often be more effective.

Activity 8 Once the presentations are over feedback from other students can be used to help the student write an assessment of her/his own performance and to set targets for improvement.

Check your learning This is a consolidation activity to check that students have understood the key elements required of a good presentation. You could ask for volunteers who are willing to give their presentation to students in a linked primary school.

Outcomes

In this chapter your students have learned how to:

- plan and structure a presentation
- select a range of vocabulary to interest and engage an audience
- use stimuli such as visual aids to make a presentation interesting
- give detailed answers to questions.

AO focus

English and English Language AO1 Speaking and listening

- Listen and respond to speakers' ideas, perspectives and how they construct and express their meanings.

- Interact with others, shaping meanings through suggestions, comments and questions and drawing ideas together.

In this chapter your students will:

- take part in discussions by making comments, asking questions and drawing ideas together

- listen and respond to other people's ideas.

Additional resources

Worksheets

26a: Putting it together

Getting started

The focus of this chapter is to develop the skills for working in groups. Students will consolidate what they have learned about what good speakers do, what good listeners do and then develop ways of sharing ideas and agreeing and disagreeing in order to foster good group work and collaborative working.

As an activity to raise students' awareness of group interaction you could ask students to draw up a list of all the groups in which they function, for example, family groups, groups of friends, sports teams etc. This could be followed up by asking students to note three things about the ways their different groups share ideas. A whole class discussion could then take place to draw out some of the skills of discussing ideas in groups.

Working through the chapter

Being a good group member

🎬 Learning activity: Positive group work

Activity 1 Here are possible ways in which students might match up the statements with the positive contributions to group work:

Possible matches	
1. Making suggestions	a, b, c, e
2. Expressing a point of view	d
3. Asking questions	f, g
4. Drawing the ideas together	h, i
5. Supporting the views of others	j, k
6. Challenging the views of others	l, m

These are not definitive answers; students may have valid alternatives. If appropriate, the statements could be displayed in the classroom as prompts during group activities.

Asking the right questions

🎬 Video case study activity: An interview

Activity 2 You may already have touched on the use of open and closed questions in Chapter 24, Activity 5. If so, this would be a good opportunity to ask students what they remember about them. Once students have prepared their lists of questions, they could work with a partner to check whether they are open or closed questions. It should be stressed that there is a place for closed questions for example, when confirming statements or perhaps at the conclusion of an interview.

Activity 3 The purpose of this activity is to provide students with the opportunity to practise the skills of being both speaker and listener/interviewer. You may wish to introduce a third student who will act as an observer to make a note of the types of questions asked. The observer (if used) and the student who was being questioned will be asked to give feedback. They should be asked to give reasons to support their answers when assessing the usefulness of the questions. Once feedback has been taken from the students who were on the receiving end of the questions you could ask the pair or the group to produce a poster entitled 'Why Good Questions Are Important'.

Working with others

🎬 Video case study activity: Group work roles

🎬 Analysis activity: Group behaviour

This section helps to alert students to some of the challenges of working in groups. It may be useful at this point to refer back to the guidelines for working in groups that they drew up at the beginning of this chapter. If necessary they could be encouraged to expand on those in response to the bulleted ideas in this section.

If you intend to appoint a chairperson to the group, then the following guidelines may be useful to students. The role of the chairperson is to:

- ensure the group is kept on task and keeps to time limits
- enable discussion of each suggestion for improvements
- make sure everyone in the group has their say
- summarise the different ideas put forward by the group
- make sure a decision is reached.

In addition to electing a chairperson to guide a group through activities and keep them on task, it can also be useful to appoint an observer. The role of the observer should be to make note of the positive features of interaction. For example:

- One student drawing another into the discussion.
- One student praising the contribution of another.
- Making a point which takes the discussion in another direction.

Activity 4 This activity provides students with the opportunity to put into practice what they have learned so far about working in a group. For some students, challenging or disagreeing with others while showing respect can be difficult. Providing such students with useful 'stock' phrases could be useful, such as:

'I understand your point, but I can't really agree with it...'

'Do you think that is always the case?'

You could also ask each group to summarise their points for presentation to the rest of the class. After the discussion you could ask students as a group to reflect on their performance using the following as a checklist:

- Did we manage to cover a range of points in the discussion?
- How well did we respond to the points made by others?
- How did we challenge the ideas of others?
- How easy or difficult was it for us to reach agreement?

You may wish students to record their reflections in the speaking and listening portfolio they began in Chapter 24.

Putting it together

Students can use their feedback from the previous activity to improve their group working skills in the next activity. Worksheet 26a can be used with this activity.

The speech bubbles about the Coleridge Centre are intended to stimulate ideas for the group activity. As a preliminary activity you could ask pupils to work in pairs and to share their reactions to the comments made and to make notes on them. You may also ask them to add some more ideas of their own.

Activity 5 In order to keep the students on task it is useful to set very clear time limits. Ensure that they are clear about the focus of the discussion as outlined in the first two bullet points. It may be helpful to point out that their discussion should cover three areas:

- Response to the statements.
- Alternative viewpoints expressed by young people.
- Suggestions for ensuring the shopping centre can be used by all age groups.

When students have collected their ideas with a partner, allocate them to groups. Avoid allowing partners who have already discussed the speech bubbles to work in the same groups as this might stifle discussion or lead to repetition of points already made.

The importance of planning as a prelude to good discussion should be stressed. Students should be allowed a maximum of ten minutes to write down their ideas in note form before the group discussion begins. Alternatively this could be set as a homework task to allow more time for reflection and consolidation.

Before beginning the discussion, allocate an extra person to join each group in the role of observer. Give them a specific task and ask them to make notes: one could look at listening skills in one group, another could look at speaking performance, another could note how the members of the group agree and/or disagree with one another. At the end of the allotted discussion time, about ten to fifteen minutes, ask the observer to report back to the group and to list strengths and weaknesses.

Now take feedback on the points made by the groups about how the Coleridge Centre might address the issue of teenagers in the centre. Ask one group to start and then encourage other groups to make points, ask questions or express opinions on what they have heard.

Review and reflect

Student responses here should be recorded in their speaking and listening portfolio together with two targets for improvement.

Check your learning At this point observers could be asked to report back on what they have noticed about their groups. Ask them to list strengths and areas for development, with examples. For example, 'Members of my group were very supportive of each other and said things like "yes", "I agree" or "absolutely" when others made points.'

Plenary

As a plenary activity you could ask students to score their skills as follows:

3 stars – very confident, 'I have good group working skills.'

2 stars – confident, 'but I still need to work on one or two areas.'

1 star – lacking confidence, 'I need to develop my skills and my confidence in working in groups.'

The students' scores could be indicated by a show of hands. If students close their eyes for fifteen seconds their response will be known only to them and the teacher.

Outcomes

In this chapter your students have:

- revised the features of good speaking and listening skills
- practised appropriate ways to agree and disagree with each other
- reflected on their skills of working in a group
- practised planning for discussion.

27 Role play

AO focus

English and English Language AO1 Speaking and listening

- Speak [to communicate] clearly and purposefully; structure and sustain talk, adapting it to different situations and audiences; use Standard English and a variety of techniques as appropriate.
- Create and sustain different roles.

In this chapter your students will learn how to:

- create a character/role
- plan and prepare the scene
- rehearse and present the scene.

Additional resources

Worksheets

27a: Playing a character

Getting started

The first section introduces students to the term 'role play' and makes them aware of what is needed to create a convincing character. As a starter activity, you could ask students to note down on sticky notes three things they understand about the term 'role play'. Their ideas could be put on a class notice board and could form the basis of a whole class discussion. As students progress through the activities they could add to their ideas.

Working through the chapter

What is role play?

The bullet points introduce students to the features they will have to consider when creating a character. In order to help students think creatively about characters, you could provide pairs of students with a photograph from a magazine or colour supplement and ask them to ascribe characteristics to their character following the bullet points in the list, i.e. background, personality and motivation. They could then present their character to another pair of students.

Activity 1 This activity enables students to focus on the use of body language and gesture as an indicator of mood and emotion. Before

beginning the activity you could act out several different moods for the students and ask them to guess which one you are acting out.

a Students will use some of the gestures illustrated in the Student Book but may have other suggestions. For example:

- Surprise: lifting hands into the air
- Anger: hunched shoulders, tensing of whole body
- Sadness: staring blankly, head in hands
- Pleasure: clapping hands, jumping up and down.

b Other facial expressions or gestures used to show feelings could include:

- Hands raised in the air: celebration
- Patting someone on the back: congratulation
- Turning back on someone: annoyance
- Shaking or nodding head: agreement/disagreement.

c When trying out different tones of voice for the listed words students may feel more comfortable doing so with a partner.

You may wish to model for them changes in volume and intonation when experimenting with the phrases 'what', 'no', 'not really' and 'goodbye'.

For example, the word 'no' could alter in volume when expressing anger, sadness, sarcasm or horror.

d Students could work with a partner for this activity taking it in turns to guess which of the bullet points is being exemplified. They could then perform their work for another pair of students to compare interpretations.

e The role play activity could also be performed for the whole class by those students who are confident enough to do so.

Following this activity, students could list for classroom display three key points they have learned about using facial expressions and gestures to create a convincing character.

Planning a role play

(kↄ) Analysis activity: Characters of the imagination

(kↄ) Analysis activity: Finding characters

(kↄ) Audio role-play activity: Hot-seating a character

At this point you may wish to revise with your students some key points about improvisation:

- Notes or a script are never used.

- Students need to think about their character before beginning the improvisation; it should not be entirely spontaneous.

- Students must listen carefully to what the other performers say and respond to them.

- Students need to stay within the role they are creating.

Creating a character

Enabling the students to think about a character before they take part in an improvisation is essential to ensure success in conveying a convincing character.

Some suggestions students could make are in the table below.

Activity 2

a You may decide to allocate students to groups based on your knowledge of their strengths and weaknesses. Alternatively you could allocate students to groups using a random number system, all those with number 1 in the same group etc. Allowing students to select their own groups does not always result in the best work.

Students should begin by sharing ideas for developing the character of the shoplifter.

b Their decisions on the role of the shoplifter will inform their ideas for developing the

characters of the store manager and the police officer. Students should be encouraged to use their own ideas for all of the characters. Some may wish to use the outline in the table, whereas others may wish to make the shoplifter someone of their own age.

c Recording their ideas on the table will assist them in creating their role. Worksheet 27a may be helpful for them to record their ideas.

Planning the scene

Planning how the scene will develop builds on the character planning the students have just completed. Before they begin, you may wish to remind students of the skills of group discussion and collaboration they have practised in Chapter 26.

It is also important to encourage them to think carefully about each of the features as outlined in the bullet points.

Activity 3 This provides an outline structure for students to use to begin to build their performance. Explaining their outline to another group may give the students feedback in the form of confirmation or in suggestions for improvement.

Character table				
Character	Background	Personality	Motivation	Feelings and attitudes
Shoplifter	• unemployed • short of money • single parent	• caring mother/father • proud – finds it hard to ask for help • normally law abiding	• desperate • child about to start primary school • wants the best for child	• feeling isolated • frightened • ashamed • worried about what people may think
Store manager	• recently promoted • first day in job as store manager • under 30, unmarried	• ambitious • seen by colleagues as insensitive	• wants to impress his bosses	• not as confident as he appears • slightly aggressive
Police officer	• has been patrolling this part of the city for years • is very experienced in dealing with crimes such as shoplifting • grandfather	• kind • generous • good sense of humour	• wants to be seen as a police officer who is sensitive to the needs of both victims and criminals	• has a strong sense of justice

Outline structure	
Audience	Students need to be encouraged to think about how their audience will affect the language they use as well as their choice of facial expressions and gesture. For example, gestures will need to be more pronounced if they are performing to a larger group.
Purpose	The message students wish to put across may vary according to the audience they have selected. For example, if performing to a group of younger students they may wish to emphasise the message 'stealing is always wrong whatever the circumstances'.
Structure	Deciding the outline of events – the beginning, middle and the end will give students the confidence to develop their ideas within the structure. More confident groups may create a surprise for the audience at the end.

The exemplar explanation of one group's plan provides students with a model against which they can review their own response to audience, purpose and structure.

Rehearsal is useful to help refine the finished product. Note that improvisation may also benefit from some run-throughs to clarify entrances/exits, dramatic moments, timing, etc.

Preparing for your own role play

At this stage students will put into practice what they have learned so far. They will be able to use the feedback from their responses to the 'Review and Reflect' to improve their performance in Activity 4.

Activity 4 It would be helpful to give students clear time limits for the role play as otherwise they sometimes produce overlong pieces lacking in dramatic tension. Five minutes should be sufficient.

a Students should be encouraged to consider the merits of each choice carefully before making their decision. They should think about:

- How successfully they played the role of an adult in the previous task, if both are comfortable in the role of an adult they may wish to opt for option 2.

- How easy or difficult it is to role play a character who is similar to them in age and experience as in option 1.

- If option 4 is adopted which character would be more appropriate for the student role – a bully, a victim or a concerned friend?

- Which option in their opinion offers the most potential for keeping the interest of an audience?

b Once again, planning is crucial to the success of this task. When completing the character plan students should think about how to create contrasts between the characters and how to build some tension into the scene.

c The chosen purpose for the role play will to some extent help students to decide on the audience. For example:

- They may choose to entertain an audience of their own age in option 1 where two friends are talking about breaking up with a girl or boy friend.

- Option 2, two parents discussing concerns about a child's behaviour could be used to inform adults about some of the pressures experienced by young people; for example, peer influence or drug taking.

d It should be stressed that deciding on the key points will help to plan the structure. They should be encouraged to think about what will make their scene interesting for an audience and however brief the role play, to have an introduction to set the scene, development and a resolution.

Review and reflect

Students should be encouraged to seek feedback from the rest of their group when completing the first **four** questions in this section. They may wish to ask for feedback from another group to measure the success they achieved in conveying their key points and in determining a positive reaction from the audience.

As with earlier activities, student reflections on their performances can be recorded in their speaking and listening portfolio.

Practice makes perfect!

It could be useful to students to rehearse their role play in front of another pair of students so that they can receive some feedback on how clearly they speak, how well they are able to vary their tone of voice to show feelings and how well they use body language.

Activity 5

a Once the rehearsal is over students should present their role play to students other than the ones with whom they rehearsed. Some students enjoy performing to the whole class and may wish to offer their role play for whole class discussion and analysis. This is recommended for students who are strong performers so that the class can concentrate on the positive aspects of their role play.

b Partners giving feedback using the checklist provided in the Student Book should be encouraged to give reasons to justify their comments. It may be helpful to students if you could model some appropriate feedback statements. For example:

'The character of the bully was well developed because in your role play you showed that he had two sides to his personality. You made it clear that he was a shy person lacking in self-esteem who was trying to make friends and impress his peers by acting as a bully. In a way his behaviour was self-defence against being bullied himself.'

Review and reflect

Along with responses and scores in Activity 5, students could record their targets in the speaking and listening portfolio. They could also measure their performance against the self-assessment they carried out after Activity 3.

A final thought

You may wish to introduce this section of the chapter at a later date and at an appropriate time in the course to support the study of written texts – either prose, poetry or drama – to assist students in exploring themes, emotions and character development.

The activities outlined in this section can be used as practice for the controlled assessment Test.

Activity 6 The activities in (a) and (b) could be tackled as group or partner activities with the purpose of enabling students to share their knowledge about the text.

The preparation activities will be familiar to students who have already completed previous sections of this chapter. Indeed when students are ready to prepare and deliver their monologue as outlined in sections (c) and (d) they should have considerable confidence and expertise as a result of their previous practice.

As in earlier activities, rehearsal time with a partner who will give feedback based on the guidelines in (c) will help students to improve their performance. Feedback from a partner after the performance can be recorded in the speaking and listening portfolio.

Plenary

Check your learning This is a consolidation activity to check that students have understood the key elements required of this sort of performance.

You may wish to introduce this before tackling the monologues.

Outcomes

In this chapter your students have:

- practised using facial expressions and gestures to help create a character
- reflected on how to build a successful character in a role play
- planned and produced role plays where they interact with others
- reflected on their own performance in role plays.

28 Making your speaking and listening skills count in the controlled assessment

AO focus

English and English Language AO1 Speaking and listening

- Speak [to communicate] clearly and purposefully; structure and sustain talk, adapting it to different situations and audiences; use Standard English and a variety of techniques as appropriate.

- Listen and respond to speakers' ideas and perspectives, and how they construct and express meanings.

- Interact with others, shaping meanings through suggestions, comments and questions and drawing ideas together.

- Create and sustain different roles.

In this chapter your students will:

- learn about how speaking and listening fits into their GCSE course

- explore the Assessment Objectives for Speaking and listening

- look at the types of task and how to respond to them.

Getting started

As a starter activity (and before looking at Chapter 28) you could ask students, either working alone or with a partner, to complete this sentence:

Speaking and listening is important at GCSE because …

Answers students might give are as follows:

- It counts towards your final marks at GCSE (some may even remember it is 20%).

- People will judge you on your speaking and listening skills when you go for job or college interviews.

- You will be more confident when you leave school if you have good speaking and listening skills.

- Being good at speaking and listening will help you with other subjects at GCSE, for example, when giving a presentation in a Science class or explaining your work to the teacher or other students in an Art class.

Working through the chapter

What is controlled assessment?

Some teachers may wish to look at this section of the chapter briefly with students at the beginning of the GCSE course when they are explaining all of the requirements to them. However, the most appropriate time to work through the tasks in detail would be when students have practised their skills in Speaking and listening by working through the activities in Chapters 24 to 27.

It is important to stress to students that doing as well as they can in speaking and listening tasks is as important as doing well in written controlled assessment tasks. You also may want to reassure them that although the controlled assessment tasks are formal assessments they can be repeated if desired.

Introducing the tasks

At this point you could ask students to reflect on what each of these tasks entails and how well they have done in them so far.

Questions the students could be asked:

- What skills do you need to be an effective presenter?

- Which presentations have you taken part in so far?

- How well do you think you did?

The word presentation/presenter would be replaced with discussing and listening or role play as appropriate.

You will now need to explain to students that they are going to look in detail at the assessment objectives (skills).

The assessment objectives will need to be clarified and exemplified for the students so that they can develop full understanding before they take part in a controlled assessment task. In answering the following questions students will also be revising and refreshing their knowledge of the skills they have already used in activities throughout the chapter.

Students could work with a partner to answer the following questions:

Speak to communicate: Show you can use language, tone of voice and body language to express your ideas.

An example of when I did this was …

Students could be asked to refer back to role-play
tasks or presentations for their examples.

Clearly and purposefully: Be clear in what you
say and make sure you achieve what you set out to.

*It is important to be clear in what you say
because …*

Here you would expect students to be thinking
about the needs of their audience.

Structure and sustain: Organise and develop your
ideas.

The best way to be organised in what you say is …

Developing your ideas means …

Students should be reminded here that planning
for speaking and listening tasks is the best way to
be well organised. As guidance in development
of ideas you could remind students that saying at
least three things about each point they make will
help them to sustain their points.

**Adapting it to different situations and
audiences**: Change what you say and how you say
it to suit your audience and purpose.

*You need to alter the way you say things to different
audiences because …*

Here you may need to remind students that in
speaking activities, just as in writing, they need
to keep a constant awareness of the needs of
audience and purpose.

Standard English: Make sure you use Standard
English when appropriate.

It is appropriate to use Standard English when …

You would expect students to remember that
Standard English is used in formal situations. You
could direct them toward the definitions in Chapter
25 on page 170.

Variety of techniques: Use repetition, rhetorical
questions, pausing for emphasis and other
techniques to make your talk more effective.

*When you are talking you need to use a variety of
techniques because …*

You would expect students to explain that these
all help to make talk more interesting and make
important points stand out.

**Listen and respond to speakers' ideas and
perspectives:** To exemplify this you could ask
students to name at least three ways in which they
indicate that they are active listeners. For example:

- asking questions
- asking a speaker to clarify a point
- challenging a point
- interpret a speaker's meaning from their tone of
  voice, gestures or their vocabulary.

Interact with others: In order to revise their skills
in a short task you could give students a title for
discussion, for example 'Homework serves no
useful purpose' and allow them three minutes with
a partner to list five points they could make.

Create and sustain different roles: Here students
could share ideas on the most memorable characters
that have been created in classroom role plays. These
need not be characters they have created themselves,
indeed they are likely not to be. Following this,
students could be asked to identify the strategies
used to create the memorable characters.

Activity 1 Students may find it helpful to work
with a partner to identify the skills they are best at,
as sometimes they can underestimate themselves.
Following this they may then identify three skills
they wish to improve on.

Activity 2 An alternative to this activity could
be to ask students to write their own definitions
before checking them with the answers below:

Answers	
1	f) Organisation
2	e) Vocabulary
3	a) Standard English
4	d) Response to questions
5	b) Participation
6	c) Role play

The tasks

(*k!*) Connecting comments activity: Effective group
work

(*k!*) Planning activity: Planning a presentation

(*k!*) On your marks activity: Role play

You may not wish to refer to all of these exemplar
tasks in one lesson. You could select the area to
be tested in the controlled assessment task, for
example, 'presentation' and focus your discussion
on this one area.

Activity 3 In addition to highlighting tasks in which
they have done best you could also ask students to
talk to their partner about how they prepared for
these tasks. The purpose of this is to reinforce for
students that successful work is always preceded by
thorough preparation.

Thinking about assessment

For this task it would be helpful to students to provide them with copies of the student record sheet as they appear in the Student Book so that they can highlight relevant comments.

Activity 4 Before students tackle part a) you may wish to show them the record sheets and ask them to work out for themselves which student has achieved more highly. This would make a very effective whole class activity on a whiteboard.

Although the focus of the activity is on Imran's contributions you may also wish to break down some of the comments in Rashid's report.

For example:

Teacher comments for Rashid	
Teacher's comments	Interpretation
'Vocabulary quite straightforward'	This could imply that vocabulary was quite simple and could perhaps have been more varied.
'Usually appropriate to task'	This implies that at times inappropriate vocabulary was used –perhaps slang or colloquialism.
'Standard English is generally used'	The above is confirmed by this statement
'Using some detail in answers'	This implies that answers could have been more developed.
'Some useful contribution to discussions'	This implies that he joined in the discussion a little but could have contributed more often.

a This table lists the comments in Imran's report which suggests he did better	
Teacher's comments	Interpretation
'Had organised what he wanted to say clearly'	This will reinforce to students that good planning before an assessment pays off.
'Vocabulary and expression showed quite good variety'	This indicates that he was aware of the need to use a range of vocabulary and expression.
'Control over and use of Standard English'	This will reinforce for students the importance of Standard English in controlled assessment tasks.
'Responses to questions showed relevant and effective detail'	This could be used to show students how giving detailed answers can help to improve their marks.
'Helpful contributions'	This suggests that he spoke appropriately and with some frequency during discussions.
'Responded appropriately'	This implies that his contributions were relevant and that he was able to follow the progress of the discussion.

b Suggested areas for Imran to improve	
Teacher's comments	Area to improve
'Expression showed quite good variety'	The use of the word 'quite' shows that this is an area to be worked on.
'Although he never led the discussion'	This suggests that he perhaps took quite a passive role and could have contributed more assertively.
'Listened closely to others and responded appropriately'	This implies that he did not add any new points to the discussion.
'Responses to questions showed relevant and effective detail'	This could be used to show students how giving detailed answers can help to improve their marks.
'Helpful contributions'	This suggests that he spoke appropriately and with some frequency during discussions.

c Once students have shared their responses with a partner you could lead a whole class discussion on how Imran could improve his performance. It is clear that his main area for improvement is in discussing and listening. Perhaps preparing more thoroughly for discussion could give him more points to contribute. Perhaps he also needs to concentrate on challenging others in an appropriate way.

Top tips

Having read and discussed all of the top tips you could ask students to spend a specified amount of time (10 to 15 minutes) selecting the ones they consider to be the most important (between five and eight approximately) to create a PowerPoint presentation to be given to another class or a poster for classroom use entitled 'Doing well in the controlled assessment test.'

Plenary

Check your learning This could form the second part of the presentation suggested above. Students' presentations to the class could form a plenary for the learning in this chapter.

Outcomes

In this chapter your students have learned:

- which tasks they will be required to prepare for the controlled assessment test
- which skills they will need to develop to do well
- how to improve their performance.

Section D: Spoken language

Overview

Section D of the Student Book is designed to develop students' skills in spoken language as defined by the Assessment Objectives for GCSE English Language (AO2 Study of spoken language) and tested in the controlled assessments.

GCSE English Language: AO2 Study of spoken language

- Understand variations in spoken language, explaining why language changes in relation to contexts.
- Evaluate the impact of spoken language choices in their own and others' use.

The chapters provide opportunities for students to develop their skills in an area generally not studied at an earlier stage in an English course. The learning objectives, founded in the Assessment Objectives but in 'student-friendly' language, are given at the start of each chapter. Throughout each chapter the learning points are clarified and modelled, and followed by activities which are designed to reinforce and extend students' learning.

Students are encouraged to work independently or in pairs or small groups, as appropriate, and are given regular opportunities to assess their personal progress and that of other students, often against fixed criteria. While many of the activities are exploratory, the learning within the chapters is designed to be cumulative, building on what has come before.

Each chapter can be used as a discrete stand-alone topic with activities and tasks specific to the named objectives. They do not have to be done in the order in which they appear in the Student Book, though it is worth noting that this order was arrived at after careful consideration of how best to build students' skills in the study of spoken language.

Assessment

GCSE English Language

Controlled assessment: Spoken language study (up to 3 hours).

Nelson Thornes resources

Chapter	Student Book activities	kerboodle! resources
29: Understanding the influences	1–2: Selecting features of spoken language and vocabulary to use in a particular context 3: Identifying features of dialect ` 4: Group discussion on accents 5: Exploring family influences on spoken language 6: Exploring the influences of social groups on spoken language 7: Examining your own idiolect Check your learning: Recording speech in a transcript	• Worksheet 29a: Purpose and audience • Worksheet 29b: How place affects the way you speak • Analysis activity: Context • Viewpoints activity: Accent and dialect • Analysis activity: Researching dialects • Webquest activity: Local dialect • Audio role-play activity: A personal way of speaking • Learning activity: Different word, same meaning
30: Multi-modal talk	1: Understanding words linked to technology Speaking and listening: Group discussion to establish conventions of texting 2: Writing a guide to texting in the 21st century 3–4: Identifying features of phone conversations 5: Identifying features of instant messaging 6: Pair or group discussion about the dangers of online chat rooms Check your learning: Preparing an advice sheet for older people on how to use texting and online messaging safely	• Worksheet 30a: Texting • Learning activity: Asking questions • Learning activity: The language of texting • Analysis activity: Spoken versus written language • Learning activity: Written and spoken English
31: Making your spoken language study skills count in the controlled assessment	1: Rewriting an extract from a sample answer on social attitudes to spoken language to take in teacher's comments 2: Analysing the language used in a sample answer on spoken genres	• Worksheet 31a: The power of words • Progress tracking: Social attitudes to spoken language tasks • Progress tracking: 'Spoken genres' task • Study skills: Planning your task response

Student checklist worksheet

Use the questions below to assess your spoken language skills and to set your personal spoken language targets.

Skill	Very confident	Quite confident	Sometimes I can't	Often I can't	Which chapters might help?
Identify different types of speech					29
Identify features of spoken language					29
Write a transcript					29
Explain how speech is influenced by purpose and audience					29
Understand the impact of technology on spoken language					29, 30
Identify different genres of spoken language					30

Use your responses to the checklist to set yourself *no more than* three targets to achieve from the Spoken language section.

1...

2...

3...

Checking students' progress

The tasks below are all included in the Student Book and can be used to check student progress in a particular skill.

Chapters	AO focus	Suggested strategies
29	Understand variations in spoken language, explaining why language changes in relation to contexts. Evaluate the impact of spoken language choices in their own and others' uses.	**Chapter 29, Check your learning** **Students:** • identify key features of a transcript • write at least ten lines of a conversation between themselves and a partner using the conventions of transcript • highlight features of their idiolect in the transcript.
30	Understand variations in spoken language, explaining why language changes in relation to contexts. Evaluate the impact of spoken language choices in their own and others' uses.	**Chapter 30, Activity 5** **Students:** • identify features of spoken and written language • decide whether they think instant messaging is a spoken or written language and give reasons for their decision • explain how participants in an instant-messaging conversation use particular linguistic and grammatical features to convey their meaning.

General resources

The resources in the Student Book, Teacher's Book and *kerboodle!* provide a range of learning opportunities for students and give them practice at developing their skills using a wide variety of text types. The resources suggested below can be used to reinforce, develop and extend students' skills and learning further.

General resources	Author and title
Further reading	**Play scripts** *England People Very Nice* by Richard Bean Excellent play text that premiered at The National Theatre earlier this year. It explores the migration to the East End of London from the base of a detention centre in the 21st century – the inmates are putting on a play about East End migration. By turns funny and sad, it explores how we are formed and how others judge us. Useful for providing an insight into the origins of language. **Poetry** *We Brits* by John Agard A satirical look at Britain from his perspective. Again, this provides a good additional slant on the origins of language and its links to culture.
Useful websites	http://news.bbc.co.uk/1/hi/magazine/default.stm – the magazine section of the BBC website often carries interesting and useful articles on the use of spoken language. www.askoxford.com – a resource based around the Oxford dictionaries, useful for 'new'/modern words added to the dictionary with some fun and interesting resources. www.bl.uk – great section here about accent/dialect. Interactive, with audio clips and regional input across the UK. http://www.bbc.co.uk/caribbean/ – the World Service's Caribbean page often has Caribbean patois based articles and might be useful for engendering interest. www.skynewstranscripts.co.uk – useful resource especially for sourcing scripts. The following websites make valuable links across the course and can be used to highlight the inter-related nature of the different areas of study. http://www.benjaminzephaniah.com/content/index.php – a performance website. www.poetryslam.org.uk – very popular with students.

29 Understanding the influences

AO focus

English Language AO2 Study of spoken language

- Understand variations in spoken language, explaining why language changes in relation to contexts.

- Evaluate the impact of spoken language choices in their own and others' use.

In this chapter your students will:

- learn about the different factors that influence the way they speak

- analyse their own individual way of speaking

- learn how to write a transcript of a conversation.

Additional resources

Worksheets

29a: Purpose and audience

29b: How place affects the way you speak

Both of these resources are designed to develop the work which is explored in the chapter. They aim to help engage students to make links between themselves and this immensely personal chapter.

Worksheet 29a is simply a series of online resources which are fun and educational; reinforcing learning and discussion which has taken place in the lesson. The links may be used during an exploratory computer lesson to gather general information, or in a more closely focused setting to gather research information for controlled assessment preparation.

Worksheet 29b is designed to give the students confidence to write up the activity about their own dialect, as well as developing preparation and delivery skills for Speaking and listening activities.

Getting started

This is an interesting chapter where the students may quickly develop a sense of ownership. Exploring the way in which we communicate as individuals is necessarily personal. However, it is essential that they understand what it is that they are exploring. That is what the activities

are designed to encourage. They are a way of accessing the knowledge which the student already possesses and enabling them to develop communication and study skills that enable them to share this information.

Start by asking the students for different situations where language might change. For example, with friends, at home, in an interview, etc. This will start them thinking about the importance of different uses of language in different situations. Further enhance their experience by allowing them to role play and explore certain situations more fully. You could use the first activity as a basis for this role play.

Working through the chapter

Purpose and audience

These activities are fairly straightforward but they help to move the students closer towards the identification of language in context. You may use the activities to firmly establish the point that the students are recognising that our spoken language is often influenced by the context in which it is used. This may be a humorous point and you may explore as a class what might happen if an inappropriate form of communication was used in various settings.

Activity 1 You could begin by checking the students' understanding of the terminology used. This may be very simply done with a quick check around the class where students are given the opportunity to explain each suggestion. Then you could illustrate the importance of correct manner and speech by demonstrating the opposite. This may make it easier for the students to identify and correct behaviour. This could easily be completed as a light-hearted role play, which will be very visual and a great way of learning for many students. Worksheet 29a may be used with this activity.

Activity 2 Activity 1 is reinforced in this practical written task. It is not too pressurised (note the word suggestion) and therefore accessible to all. This really flags up the importance of making the link between what is being explored and being able to put ideas onto paper. In this safe environment, and utilising the enthusiasm generated by the previous task, this should be relatively straightforward.

How place affects the way you speak

(kt) Analysis activity: Context

(kt) Viewpoints activity: Accent and dialect

Be very clear about the difference between accent and dialect. The key term definitions help. Ask some students if they may mimic either a local or another regional accent. Make the point that we may speak Standard English with an accent but a dialect is made up of some non-standard words. Read the introduction to support this idea. Reading the same sentence in different accents really helps to highlight that accent is different to dialect because sounds, not word, change.

Activities 3 and 4

(kt) Analysis activity: Researching dialects

(kt) Webquest activity: Local dialect

If there is not a pronounced regional dialect in your area, students may find these activities difficult. Worksheet 29a may be helpful here. It is a general resource which points the students towards the variety of dialect in the UK. The British Library resources are particularly useful and because of their interactive nature they are user-friendly for all abilities. You may choose to use this as a specifically focused activity or enable the students to gather their own base of information by exploring these sites for themselves.

The activities based on regional accent are not only an opportunity for the class to establish how pronounced their local accent is but also to discuss the social implications of an accent. A class discussion would allow them to share their views and to understand the way that some people are influenced by the way others speak. You might ask the class whether there are any situations where a regional accent would be inappropriate. For example, reading the news, giving a speech, etc. Remember to approach such discussions with caution and always to be aware of any students who may feel that this is too personal for them.

How family affects the way you speak

(kt) Learning activity: A personal way of speaking

Establish that we owe much of the way we speak to the influence of our parents, our home and the environment in which we live. Make the point that we often have many options for saying the same thing and that we often use particular options according to what we have picked up at home. This is also a good point to introduce the concept of how we consciously alter how we speak (including both accent and dialect words)

in different circumstances. You may be aware of people who have 'telephone voices' or a regional accent which comes out when they meet up with other people from that area. This is also something which the students will observe more easily for themselves when they start to realise what is around them. It may provide a good basis for discussion and exploration.

You could use these examples:

'We had a pleasant evening' or 'We had a good night out'.

'Where is the lavatory?' or 'Where is the toilet?'

Activity 5 Once you have established the point that home life is an influence, introduce Activity 5. Work through a couple of examples with the class then allow the students to work in groups to complete the activity. Take feedback and broaden the discussion to incorporate part b) of the activity. Ask the class to address the issue of 'correctness'. Is it more correct to say 'toilet' rather than 'bog', for example? Open up the whole idea of appropriateness and the circumstances in which we establish 'appropriate' patterns of speech.

How social groups affect the way you speak

(kt) Learning activity: Different word, same meaning

Establish the point that young people often experiment with language and many of our words have been introduced by young people. Read the introduction to this section. You might add your own list of words or expressions introduced through the youth culture and now widely used – for example, 'gig', 'no way' or 'solid'. It is interesting to establish (using the students as the experts) why they use this language – what is it that attracts them? Indeed, is it because some adults react to it in a negative way that makes it so very interesting to them?

As an additional activity, you may wish to explore recent additions to the Oxford English Dictionary; much of this will be considered 'modern' speech which has found its way into the dictionary through common usage. Please see the additional resources section in the Introduction for suggested links which may illustrate clearly how the English language is a living, growing organism.

Activity 6 Now allow the students to tackle Activity 6. Take feedback. Identify differences in usage within the class. Then you may wish to renew the discussion about correctness (part b). At this point students often respond well to a discussion about the context in which it is appropriate/inappropriate to use 'youth speak'. This activity will further develop the discussion about why they choose to use certain words and forms of language. It is important to have the confidence to let the students speak and express themselves in a controlled environment which encourages free speech. In this way, they will be able to add a great deal to their own and the rest of the class's knowledge and understanding.

How do you speak?

Activity 7 This is an opportunity for students to pull together all they have learned in this section in order to analyse their own idiolect. The secret to success here is the teacher input. Start by using some of your own information about your idiolect to model how to complete this exercise. Allow students some time to complete this. It might be useful to allow students to use a partner as a sounding board. For example: 'Do you think I use lots of youth speak language? Is my accent strong, would you say?' Having explored why they use language in this way, and the effect which it has on others, will enable them to explore more fully their own idiolect and be able to make informed statements about the way they speak and why. Again, this is an important learning tool; enabling them to speak freely about themselves and their own speech.

Recording how you speak

This may be unfamiliar territory to students and teachers alike. However, what initially appears to be daunting is actually a rich vein of reference and may provide excellent material for analysis if approached in the correct manner. A useful approach may be to source a simple transcript which illustrates conventions and gives a simple overview of the format required. It is a good idea to run through this with the group on a whiteboard or other interactive facility, illustrating the conventions and demonstrating the transcript as a source for analysis. Transcripts are available on the internet or you may choose to create your own.

At a later point you may choose to provide a transcript for the whole class as a controlled assessment task or you may choose to offer a choice to your students. Either way, you must ensure that they have sufficient detail to actually analyse. A lack of material may make an otherwise straightforward task rather frustrating and limiting.

Plenary

Check your learning You can set this task up by reading it aloud in several different ways; placing stress in different places depending on how it is punctuated. Giving the students a short set amount of time (depending on ability) will really help to focus their concentration and recall of learning. Sharing results is always good fun!

Outcomes

In this chapter your students have:

- understood the influences on a person's idiolect

- understood the key terms: idiolect, dialect, accent, Standard English, sociolect, transcript

- actively participated in discussion of some of the factors that affect spoken English

- actively participated in reflective paired discussion about their own idiolect

- written a reflection on how their own idiolects have been influenced by their experiences

- understood the conventions of writing about their own language choices.

30 Multi-modal talk

AO focus

English Language AO2 Study of spoken language

- Understand variations in spoken language, explaining why language changes in relation to contexts.
- Evaluate the impact of spoken language choices in their own and others' use.

In this chapter your students will:

- learn about the impact of technology on spoken language
- identify the features of texting
- consider the relationship between instant messaging and spoken language
- discuss the dangers and advantages of instant messaging.

Additional resources

Worksheets

30a: Texting

This worksheet is designed to focus the students on the subject of writing guides and engage them with thinking about audience and purpose. It may also be used as a trigger task for other written tasks which will be useful for the rest of the syllabus.

Getting started

Ask your students to look at the word 'multi-modal' and think about what it means. You will need to lead this learning by making links to other words which have the same root. Encourage students to find the way in – especially with the much used 'multi' – multiplex cinemas, multicoloured, multi-tasking, etc. Modal may be introduced by talking about different ways of doing things – different modes. This task opens their minds up to language and the deeper ideas of word meanings. This is useful for students of all abilities as it allows them to focus and 'own' their work. It becomes more of a game of linking than a task which uses complex and 'new' language.

Then you may ask them to discuss the meaning of multi-modal – perhaps make a list of their answers – and make a list of the most helpful ones for the classroom wall as a point of reference. To help with the discussion it may be useful to collate a list of as many multi-modal forms of communication as possible, which could also be put up on the wall. This gives a good overview of the area of study and opens up possibilities for both the teacher and the students.

Working through the chapter

The impact of technology

kt Learning activity: Asking questions

The purpose of this chapter is to enable students to engage fully with the concept of multi-modal talk. This is new territory for many teachers and very much the world of the student, which is good news as it will enable students to have a real sense of ownership and begin to explore further. It is an interesting topic which has many uses and may be developed and explored in many ways. It is also a fast-evolving area and this may be a good opportunity to really involve the students as the 'experts' at the cutting edge of technology. This will pay dividends in all chapters as they become involved more fully in their learning and as they begin to understand that learning is the sharing and developing of knowledge and that teachers are not simply there to impart information.

Activity 1 This is a recap activity to ascertain understanding before the students move on to the main body of the lesson. It will build on the starter activity and use the focus which they have already begun to explore by further unpicking the term 'multi-modal'. This enables them to engage with the language which is used to explore the concepts and begin to become more familiar with the sorts of ideas which will be discussed, including the vocabulary used. Again, this is all knowledge which is readily available to them but which has probably not been discussed to this detail in an educational setting before.

Sharing will reinforce clarity.

Texting

kt Learning activity: The language of texting

This Speaking and listening activity is a good way of engaging the students with an analytical process which they will need to adopt for their GCSE course. It covers group working skills of speaking and listening and encourages them to interact with each other, building on and developing ideas to establish the 'rules' and conventions of texting. This is a chapter activity which may also be used as part of their collection of work for the 'interacting and responding' section of the Speaking and listening assessment. This is the sort of chapter activity which may be easily used to develop links using Speaking and listening activities in order to illustrate the connected nature of these tasks.

Activity 2 This activity uses Worksheet 30a.

This activity involves the student in an analysis of something which is commonplace. This encourages them to think much more deeply about what they are doing when they text and how this may be explained to other people. Each activity in the chapter builds on its predecessor to reinforce learning and makes the students more aware of everyday life as a source of analysis. It encourages them to look repeatedly at what they take for granted because it will provide a rich basis for later analysis. It is very rewarding when students become more aware of everyday activity and start to notice more of what is going on in the world around them. This leads to numerous comments about language use and different people in different situations as well as where texting and messaging are used and by whom. All of this is great news as it means that the students are really engaging with their learning and showing ownership.

Worksheet 30a is of use here, offering ideas about the language, tone and style of differing guides and also developing an awareness of audience. The introduction of a more focused written element at this point is important as it enables both students and teacher to begin to focus discussion and note work into a more structured written task, which will, in turn, lead into the controlled assessment task itself.

Talking on the telephone

🔲 Analysis activity: Spoken versus written language

🔲 Learning activity: Written and spoken English

Activity 3 This activity widens the focus again by encouraging students to explore the differences and similarities between texting and telephone conversations. While appearing to be easy, it has the intention of opening up their thinking to engage with the 'how' of multi-modal communication. This activity continues to build up the layers of understanding so that the students are constantly being given more detailed knowledge of the chapter areas in order to make an informed and interesting decision when it comes to completing their controlled assessment task. Awareness is all important here. This whole task is about noticing and being able to comment on what is going on in the world around them.

Activity 4 This continues to develop a depth of ownership and analysis, building notes and understanding of previously explored work. It makes the students increasingly more aware of the details which are so important and yet barely registered in everyday life. This is a further opening up of their critical awareness which gives them the ability to act and think in a focused manner when it comes to selecting a subject for their final controlled assessment task.

'Talking' online

Activity 5 This activity is designed to consolidate what has been discovered so far, and then reach further into the concepts of multi-modal communication. It clarifies the differences between different modes of communication and the overlap in the multi-modal realm. This should fully consolidate the students' learning up to this point. Students are now in a very strong position to think about personal decisions regarding their choice of focus for the controlled assessment task.

The dangers of talking too much

Activity 6 This activity has a dual purpose. It is designed to generate a class discussion and to generate a real awareness of the problems which there are online. Many students are so happy and at home in the world of technology that they are unaware of the many dangers which anonymity on the web affords people with inappropriate intentions. This activity creates a safe environment in which to open up this important topic. It also creates some interesting cross-over points which can be used in conjunction with the teaching of the non-fiction based chapters. This provides the ability to cross-relate activities and create a whole teaching approach which enables tasks to inter-relate to each other, rather than simply standing alone. This is something which more easily mimics the world of work and will mean much more to the average student than activities and skills taught in isolation.

Check your learning This activity allows students to review all that they have discussed and explored in this chapter. The aim of the activity is to enable them to put their knowledge into words and begin to share it with an audience beyond that of their teacher and peers. It is a 'real' task which works with the idea of a practical approach which will be used by teachers to perhaps inter-relate to other courses which the student is studying, making it all the more relevant and applicable to the world in which we live.

The whole point of this chapter is to develop an awareness of modern forms of mixed-mode communication. The best way in which to make these relevant to the students of today is to apply them in a realistic learning environment where the reality of work provides the impetus for learning and the focus is on ownership and discovery.

This activity could easily be developed into a Speaking and listening activity, as well as linking to other units within the qualification. It is another point for course integration – ideal for maximising time and easing teaching constraints and also ideal for showing students the interconnected nature of this study.

Plenary

Ask the students to make clear and concise notes in preparation for the 'Check your learning' activity about sharing relevant information with older people who might not be at ease with this style of communication. This should focus them on the task and really flag up what they have learned, as well as any areas which they may need to do some work on.

Outcomes

In this chapter your students have:

- explored terminology
- applied terminology
- become more aware of multi-modal communication in the world around them
- linked personal observations to useful applications of exploring and explaining.

AO focus

English Language AO2 Study of spoken language

- Understand variations in spoken language, explaining why language changes in relation to contexts.
- Evaluate the impact of spoken language choices in their own and others' use.

In this chapter your students will:

- learn about how spoken language speaking and listening fits into their GCSE English Language course
- explore the Assessment Objectives for spoken language
- look at the types of tasks they might undertake in their controlled assessment.

Additional resources

Worksheets

31a: The power of words

Getting started

The simple starter task on Worksheet 31a may help to engage students and illustrate the power of language in a visual way. The potential differences of opinion are a perfect way of opening up discussion on the depths of meaning in words.

The second task is designed to show the power of words in a practical situation. Both statements use the same words, but they do not say the same thing. The first statement leaves the reader with a negative feeling because it starts off using negative words. The second statement is much more powerful because it starts with positive words. This reality based application statement is a good illustration of the power of vocabulary.

Working through the chapter

What is controlled assessment?

This section outlines clearly the requirements of the controlled assessment task, highlighting the many positive aspects and ensuring that the students are fully aware of the component parts of the work required by AQA. It is deliberately written to give the students a complete overview of the options but stressing that teacher knowledge is important in choosing the best setting for this task to take place. It gives a thorough insight into the nature of preparation and the importance of the task as the culmination of preparatory work which is relatively wide ranging and skills based.

Controlled assessment is an opportunity for the students to show what they know in a set amount of time without the pressure of redrafting. Students should be encouraged to enjoy the process of gathering material for their study task. It is important that students recognise the time limit that is set for the task as a positive because it will enable them to focus on the entirety of the task and break it down into manageable sections where they can effectively share and analyse the information they have gathered.

The controlled assessment will be taken in conditions which are like an exam, but without the pressure.

- Final outcomes must be completed under formal supervision in a period of up to 3 hours. These can be timetabled as appropriate.
- Brief notes will be allowed, but not drafts or essay outlines.
- Students will be allowed to bring transcripts.
- They will also be allowed to use a dictionary or thesaurus to check their work.
- The final written work should be between 800 and 1,000 words.

Completion of the work:

- You may choose to complete the research and task in a number of lessons to fit in with your timetable. If this happens then the students will not be allowed to take any work away with them; it will be kept securely until the next session.
- You may choose to allow computer access to complete the work. If this happens then the students are not allowed general access

to the internet (only to source work such as transcripts or video clips which have been stored previously) and their work will be stored on a secure server so that it cannot be accessed when they have left the room and feel the urge to carry on working!

The transcript

It is important to note that your guidance of students in this preparation work is extremely important. You may choose to source a transcript for your entire group to use (being aware of copyright restrictions) or you may allow them (with support) to produce their own. It is advisable to stress to the students the need for a **good quantity** of material in order to provide a good basis for analysis. This is something which most students find very difficult and time consuming and can detract from the assessment task itself. It may be advisable to teach the differing areas of study and gauge the interest of the group. Then you will be in a better position to target the selection of transcript material to support their controlled assessment task.

It would still be a good idea to provide a variety as this gives an element of personal learning and acknowledges that we do not all think in the same way. There are a number of transcript resources available legally online which can provide a good basis for analysis.

If students do source their own material, please warn them about copyright restrictions and remind them that they cannot record conversations without permission!

Introducing the tasks

There are three choices of topic area for the investigative spoken language study:

- Social attitudes to spoken language
- Spoken genres
- Multi-modal talk.

There will be two task options for each topic, but students only need to complete one of these.

Social attitudes to spoken language

This task deals with how we perceive language and how we react to it. It is an interesting area of study which will involve the exploration of how different people talk and how language use changes with generations and situations. Your students will be asked to choose a topic and answer only one question from the controlled assessment question

bank. The key words for this topic will be 'reflect' or 'investigate'.

Spoken genres

There are many aspects which are similar to 'Social attitudes to spoken language' in this area of study. Your students will be asked to choose a topic and answer only one question from the controlled assessment tasks. The key words for this topic will direct students to consider 'how' something is 'represented' or to 'investigate' it.

Multi-modal talk

This is an area which many students will be particularly interested in. It allows them to explore and explain about instant messaging and text speak. It is an area which is fast moving and constantly evolving. There are lots of questions that the students can ask and investigate:

- What sort of language is it? Speech? Or written language?
- Is it a mixture of both? It is written language and yet the way it is written as it sounds, is so much closer to speech.

Your students will be asked to choose a topic and answer only one question from the controlled assessment tasks. The key words for this topic will be:

- 'How', relating to the practicalities of the actual communication.
- 'What devices' is linked to this and they will be asked to link their discoveries to real speech.

They are being asked to explore the links between this written communication and how it can be considered a relation of spoken language.

Assessment Objectives

This section begins to develop an insight into the Assessment Objectives for students using 'student friendly' language. This is an ideal point for the development of these objectives by using some of the resources in the latter part of this chapter to highlight how student essays are marked and what these objectives mean in reality.

Advise students to keep the Assessment Objectives in mind when they are preparing their material:

- Show that you know why people speak in different ways at different times and in different places.
- Make comments (positive and negative) about the effects of the language which people choose to use.

Preparing for the controlled assessment – choosing a task

The sections under this heading are designed to develop the students' thought patterns and encourage them to really develop their own work and analysis. It works by introducing some of the meta-language and beginning to familiarise the students with using such terms in their comments and discussion of what they are learning. It helps to develop a skills base, which will enable students to fully engage with the requirements of the assessment.

Analysing your information

Once the students have gathered their information they need to think about the most important points which their data gives them. They will need to note different things, for example:

- Word use: how, why different words are used. Do they have different meanings in different age groups?
- Frequency of words
- Jargonized words
- Word deviations in text or MSN speak.

Sample tasks and answers

[k] Progress tracking: Social attitudes to spoken language task

[k] Progress tracking: 'Spoken genres' task

[k] Study skills: Planning your task response

The aim of this section is to give a brief generic outline which can be used to give a sense of safety when structuring essays without leading the student. It develops a relatively simple scaffold that encourages them to consider a deep response that covers a limited amount of points in good detail. This is something that students often find difficult as they are normally keen to show the breadth of their knowledge and therefore omit to explore the depth.

The exemplar essay extracts are used to highlight certain elements of responses and give a sense of the work required. They include a question analysis, response and teacher's comment to show the stages of development; moving from how to analyse a question, through response and then to the commentary which accompanies the final extract. This shows the student the good practice of question analysis and also gives them an idea of how the assessment criteria are interpreted by a marker. The idea is to generate discussion and encourage the students to think

about how they might develop such a response themselves.

Social attitudes to spoken language

Activity 1 This encourages the students to read closely and with understanding. Reading and exploring a commentary and then having to physically take action to improve the work will enable them to more easily engage with their own concepts and begin to develop the art of reviewing and drafting work. The task is designed to reach beyond simply reading into an activity that will reinforce the concepts they are reading about.

Spoken genres

Activity 2 The purpose of this task is to enable the student to engage with the power of language. It is important that the students understand these concepts and are knowledgeable about how they work for their studies in general, and particularly for this controlled assessment task.

This is a task which may be adapted to be used as a quick ten-minute starter activity with the purpose of enabling students to develop a reflex response to language analysis and moving towards a point where they will be able to demonstrate a depth of analysis with ease.

Points for analysis:

- What are the connotations of these words?
- What other words would they link to?
- Are they words which float somewhere in the middle of meaning or are their meanings very black and white?

For example:

'Enemy' is a word which conjures up many negative links; from war zones to playground disputes gone horribly wrong. It is the exact opposite to how we would really wish the world to be and leaves no real room for negotiation. It is definite in its negativity. It is a word which is dark and unambiguous. There is no danger of misinterpretation here and it can only be used in the harshest terms.

'Faithful' can apply equally to a pet dog or someone involved in worship. It is a quiet, non-aggressive word which mirrors its meaning; a soft, gentle respect. It gives a sense of longevity, being unbounded by time, something which reaches into eternity. It is a gentle, springlike word which seems to be forever youthful and simple.

The worksheet accompanying this task works to enable the students to really engage with the power of words.

Check your learning This chapter gathers a great deal of information which is known to most people, but has not been explored in terms of language and does not actually form the basis for much conversation. This is a very interesting area of study which will make many links across the rest of the course and which will be very valuable in encouraging students to 'own' their own learning and be prepared to become 'experts' in their own knowledge areas.

Plenary

You could ask the students to summarise their learning by presenting a short piece on an aspect of the work which they have covered. This does not need to be overly time consuming and will allow you to cover all aspects of the work by assigning work to students. You can enable them to focus on their strengths and encourage them to produce a good piece of work by setting it as a formal assessment point for speaking and listening.

Outcomes

In this chapter your students have:

- learned about how spoken language fits into their GCSE English Language course
- learned more about the ways they can achieve high marks in this part of the course.

English essentials

Punctuation

Activity 1 The following punctuation reflects a likely choice though students could have placed exclamation marks at the end of the final sentence.

How many times must we hear the same old argument? Teenagers always say their friends are allowed to do the things we won't allow them to. Is this really true? Yesterday, my son Chris asked if he could go to a party in Newquay and stay overnight. He said that all his friends were going. However, when I rang Maggie, his best friend's mother, she said her son had said exactly the same thing. Enough is definitely enough it's time for parents to fight back!

Commas

Activity 2 The following punctuation reflects correct usage:

Your computer can catch a virus from disks, a local network or the internet. Just as a cold virus attaches itself to a human host, a computer virus attaches itself to a program and, just like a cold, it is contagious. Like viruses, worms replicate themselves. However, instead of spreading from file to file, they spread from computer to computer infecting an entire system.

Apostrophes

Activity 3 The following punctuation reflects correct usage:

John's mother told him not to go to Peter's house during the week's holiday. However, he borrowed his brother's bike and went straight there. There was no one in, though the younger children's toys were still out on the lawn. Peter's window was open and John climbed through it to wait for him. Unfortunately, he was spotted by the neighbour's dog and then by the neighbour.

Inverted commas

Activity 4

a Students are requested to study the extract and the annotations. You may wish to do this on the whiteboard as a class activity.

b It is as though Larkin believes that 'being beautiful' is not always something to be wished and can be 'unworkable'. In contrast being 'not ugly, not good-looking' can bring greater happiness, perhaps because you put more effort into being happy. It is for this reason that he wishes she should:

'Have, like other women,

An average of talents.'

Spelling

Syllables

Activity 5 The aim of this activity is to help students to break words down. Students may have put breaks in slightly different places though likely choices are:

ab/so/lute/ly   poss/i/ble   choc/o/late

prej/ud/ice   int/er/est/ing   diff/er/ent

Suffixes

Activity 6 Students will compile lists of varied lengths. An example is:

a Wondered, wondering, wonderingly

Encourage students to swap answers to see which pair can come up with the most words.

b panic**king** traffic**king** mak**ing** dat**ing**   guarantee**ing**   slic**ing**   sitt**ing**   tapp**ing**

putting bounti**ful** play**ful** beauti**ful** challenge**able** balance**able** debat**able** pronounce**able**

barred sobb**ed** fax**ed** tann**ed** nett**ed**

Prefixes

Activity 7 The aim is to get students thinking about the use of prefixes. Once the activity is completed you could get them to check their 'new' words in a dictionary. For example:
misbehave, displace, mistrust, disorder, dishonest

Combining prefixes and suffixes

Activity 8 Again students are encouraged to 'create' words using prefixes and suffixes. One example is:

disagree

disagree**able**

disagree**ably**

disagree**ment**

disagree**ing**

disagre**ed**

Plurals

Activity 9

a branches holidays Christmases beachesladies atlases inches circuses blushes

comedies speeches takeaways hoaxes   witches berries bonuses pluses

essays gases coaches keys   blotches bullies dishes arches

b dashes crunches discs trolleys women oxen   proves babies lives axes

dominoes faxes screens halves spies lunches beliefs desks wives